D1550266

TRULY BIZARRE

Harold E. Priestley

STERLING
PUBLISHING CO., INC. NEW YORK

London & Sydney

Published in the United States of America
by Sterling Publishing Co., Inc.
Two Park Avenue, NY 10016
Published in the U.K. by Oak Tree Press Co., Inc.
Distributed by Ward Lock Ltd., 116 Baker St., London W1
Published in Australia by Oak Tree Press Co., Inc.,
660 George St., Sydney, N.S.W.
Manufactured in the United States of America
Library of Congress Catalog No. 78-68689
Sterling ISBN: 0-8069-0134-9 Trade
0135-7 Library
Oak Tree 7061-2614-9

CONTENTS

PREFACE

The word bizarre is very specific—and very demanding. An event may be interesting, even fascinating, but yet not bizarre. To qualify as bizarre something must be extreme, incredible, outrageous BUT TRUE.

The events recorded in this collection have been carefully checked and researched. However amazing or absurd, everything is factual. "Truly Bizarre" starts with pure entertainment and proves that mankind is capable of hilarious and almost unbelievable extremes. Later it investigates some mysteries that demand that the more we investigate the world's phenomena the more we must keep our minds open. Nothing, it appears, is impossible and refusal to consider the unthinkable could be positively dangerous. If there is a message in this book it is that a sense of humour and a sense of wonder are sorely needed in today's fast changing world.

January, 1979

The word bizarre is itself just a little bizarre. It is the same word in almost every language and one of the very few words to enter our speech from Basque—a tongue of the Pyrenees Mountains in northern Spain. The original word was "bizarra" which meant bearded and came to mean "eccentric and fantastic" because so few men in that district cultivated facial hair. The Basque language is different from every other language in the world and the origin of the Basque people themselves is still a mystery.

BIZARRE PERSONALITIES

BIZARRE PERSONALITIES

OUR WILDEST ECCENTRICS

Justice of the Peace Herbert Thwing of Seabournville, New Hampshire, is a seasoned veteran of the marriage service. He was not surprised therefore when a young engaged couple asked him to marry them in a balloon. He didn't mind at all.

"A balloon is dignified," he insisted. "It drifts above the earth quiet as a bird and makes a lovely place for a wedding."

The judge has married people in strange places. One was on a barge when the guests came to the ceremony by boat, another on a bridge.

These were by no means as bizarre as the wedding ceremony once conducted by Pastor Ezra Nero of the Landmark Spiritual Temple who called out the vows while he was suspended 75 feet above the congregation and the bride and bridegroom were doing a trapeze act.

Bizarre actions can often be forced on otherwise quite normal people by outside regulations. Take, for instance, the case of the violinist in the Juilliard String Quartet who was travelling by air. Violin cases are not easy things to fit under seats and he was forced by one airline to buy a ticket for the instrument. So he strapped his violin case to the seat, tied a napkin round its neck and made the stewardess serve it dinner.

Many people don't like new inventions. They feel unsure of them. Self-serving gasoline pumps are especially distrusted because the instructions are not so easy to follow. One lady drove up to one, got out of her car, looked at the instructions on the pump and then put a dollar bill into the nozzle of the hose. Annoyed that no fuel came out, she shouted down the nozzle, "Five gallons of super, please!"

Even places of learning are not exempt from the bizarre. At breakfast time at the Chichester College of Education the students were instructed to sing *God Save the Queen* while the bacon was being fried. The teacher, Mrs. Ivy Davey, explained, "*God Save the Queen* has a running time of two minutes—just long enough for each side of a rasher."

This may be worth trying at home!

The justice, the balloonists, the trapeze artists, the violinist and the college instructress were all perfectly normal people, otherwise they would never have been able to hold down their jobs. Now and again we all ought to have the pleasure of indulging our eccentricities.

Messrs. Moneybags

Giving out money for nothing is a certain way of bringing at least temporary happiness to some people. Within ten days in June, 1974, Clive Peel Oversby got rid of more than £600 ($1,200) in the English Cornish holiday resort of St. Agnes during a series of wild spending sprees.

He started by buying £2 worth of prime steak and slapped it on an ice-cream stand, saying to the astonished salesman, "You look like a man who needs a square meal."

Day after day, he would snatch cigarettes from smokers' mouths, crush them in his fist, and hand over to each smoker a pound note. He bought up the whole of a shop's stock of seaside rock and handed it out to grown-ups and children telling them, "Eat this up for your dinner." Every evening in the public houses he bought drinks all round from a seemingly limitless wad of notes. Asked to explain his motives, he said, "I like to see smiles on people's faces."

Nonetheless, the little town was very glad to see the back of him. One local summed it all up—"We can produce enough of our own nuts without importing them."

A rather more pleasant episode was one that happened one morning in September of the same year to motorists who were going to business along a main road in the North of England.

An elderly man was sitting on a chair in the rain on the back of an open lorry, scattering pieces of paper which fluttered down on to the roadway. No sooner had he finished one bundle than he fished another out of his pocket and started again.

At first the motorists following him thought the pieces of paper were old circulars or leaflets until, on picking them up, it turned out that they were £10 notes.

Mr. Geoffrey Hyde from Barnsley drove past two scattered bundles, then when the man threw out more, he stopped to investigate. Altogether he picked up £570. Others soon joined in and took differing amounts. One woman had taken £220 in £10 notes when the police arrived. Unfortunately all of the treasure-hunters had been so intent on what they were doing that nobody thought of taking the number of the lorry.

Altogether the police collected some £1,030. "You have to admire their honesty," said a spokesman. "But I wonder how many people are keeping quiet about what they found."

The money was taken away by the police, but, after two months if nobody claimed it, it could be handed back to the finders.

The police suggested that the benefactor might have been an eccentric, but on the other hand he might have been a thief anxious to get rid of some incriminating loot. Or, it could have been a person in crisis whose mind had been temporarily thrown off balance.

Nobody ever found out who the unknown benefactor was, though the police managed to trace the lorry-driver who had given him a lift. He and his mate had been rewarded with a tip of 50 pence ($1) each!

Locked in an Eternal Past

For Lawrence Broadmoore the fascination was in the past. Not history in general, though he was a former student of the subject, but one small slice of it—the year 1923. He shut himself up in the events of that year and refused to come out.

Society in the period since the Second World War had destroyed what for him were the high peaks of civilized living. For television, time-saving, computerization, space travel and everything on the new frontiers of technology he had only one expletive—balderdash!

So he grew his moustache long and waxed it, put on a winged collar, pince-nez glasses and an out-of-date suit, installing himself in a house on the Hudson without plumbing, and earned money by repairing old gramophones, pianos and all kinds of ancient household gadgets just as if he were living in the year 1923.

"I moved back to the era I admired," he said. "I live in a totally insular world, guarded from philosophical relevance (whatever that may mean!) by my own vigilance. The only people I can discuss life with today are all over 70, and they don't think the old days were all that good."

He ought to know. In 1978 he was 27 years old.

"We Want to Be Happy"

The farm of Mrs. Martin in Kent, England, is completely dominated by railway memorabilia. Almost every day Mr. and Mrs. Martin dress themselves up in authentic railway gear and operate their model line on a 1938 main line timetable, running extra services holidays and extra large horse-boxes in Royal Ascot racing week. They have to eat in shifts to maintain their self-imposed timetable.

Some people have an unquenchable desire to make others happy. Every weekday morning during rush hour Joseph W. Charles of Berkeley, California, steps to the front of his well-kept house, waves and smiles greetings to all the drivers who pass by. "The people out there enjoy it," he explained. "I can enjoy it too; it makes me feel good. My religion is in my heart."

Passers-by are probably used to it by now. But then, Mr. Charles is 68 and retired while some of the drivers are quite possibly going to spend another day in some dull office job. It is inconceivable that one of them should not occasionally see the waving figure on the tidy lawn without a twinge of envy.

Adding Spice to Life

These are not in the main bizarre personalities. They are quite ordinary kindly people who have found through imagination and sympathy an outlet and a road to happiness and fulfilment. They harm nobody and often make their own contribution to social well-being and knowledge. We should wish success to the urban cowboys, suburban spacemen and born-again Sioux Indians, for they are all part of the kaleidoscope that lends variety to life in this age of mechanization and growing uniformity.

Note, however, the difference between these and the true bizarre personality. The latter is quite often elderly, rich and powerful, a person, usually a man, who can afford to flout convention and do outrageous things.

THE MILLIONAIRE ECCENTRICS

Art with a Vengeance

Stanley Marsh, a Texan millionaire of the third generation, has the money to go his own way, writing his self-invented nickname God Bless America between his two other names, as the Puritans of Old England did—Stanley God Bless America Marsh. After attending the University of Pennsylvania he went into the family oil business, but was really much more interested in out-of-the-way art and bought a bookstore. Now he lives in Toad Hall, an elaborate stone mansion on a 10,000-acre ranch, once in the country but since the spread of the fast-growing town of Amarillo, feeling and resenting the approach of suburbia.

He has been an eccentric from his youth. When urban sprawl threatened the privacy of his family residence, he had a sign put next to the highway announcing that the world's most poisonous snake-farm was being built there.

"What is Art?" he was asked. By way of answer, he had three eight-foot-high letters A R T cut in wood, painted red, yellow and blue respectively and placed leaning against the fence in his backyard. Now, in answer to the question, he points silently at them. What does he mean?

Probably this. Art is what you yourself consider it to be. It does not exist *of itself* but depends for its existence entirely on your approach.

"Art," he says, "should be two things, surprising and hidden from people. Art has to get you out of your mental rut. And it should be far away so you can't get to see it too easily. Nothing lives up to expectations, not even the Mona Lisa which disappointed me. Nothing compares to what people dream about."

Hence, his monument commissioned in the 1950's was called the Great American Dream. That was the time when the Cadillac with its large fins reached the peak in styling. The monument consists of ten of these Cadillacs sunk halfway into the ground, hood first, on the city limits of Amarillo. Each slants alongside Route 66 towards California where the road eventually leads, and leans at the same angle to the ground as the Great Pyramid of Cheops in Egypt.

The monument was designed and executed by a group calling itself the San Francisco Art Farm and now sits forlornly in a cornfield with weeds growing around it and empty beer cans on the ground. Yet, say visitors, though most people like to make fun of it when they first see it, the longer they look at it and the more they learn about it, the more they come to visualize it as a serious art production.

One of the works Stanley G. B. A. Marsh had made for him

was the world's largest soft pool table. The original one was on a remote part of his ranch and consisted of several acres of undulating grassland with a number of huge billiard balls and a stick. Subsequently he bought a large building, the flat roof of which he had painted green and on it he had the large colorful balls placed, and the giant wooden stick by its side.

Marsh does not claim to be an artist but says he knows good art when he sees it. His latest idea is to build a hill consisting of boots, and to do this he has said (in these words): "I want every cowboy west of the Mississippi to send me his boots when he dies."

Marsh also owns a zoo and included in it are a Chinese dog with green wings tattooed on his sides "in case he wants to fly one day," and a stuffed pig.

Stuffed animals are not new to zoos. The executives of one English TV company that diversified by purchasing a zoo in Yorkshire, were proudly inspecting their new purchase the following morning. One of the party pointed out that some of the animals were unusually fond of sleeping. "Why," said the seller, "they're not sleeping. They're stuffed. The public never knows the difference because they expect many of the exhibits to be asleep—and it cuts the food costs down enormously!"

"The Wacky Millionaire"

For a rich eccentric with a reputation, Marsh, just turned 40, is still young. He has quite a long way to go yet. So has Caruth Byrd, an affable Texan distantly related to the polar explorer Admiral Richard E. Byrd and U.S. Senator Harry F. Byrd, Jr. "Of course, I'm the black sheep of the family," he says. "I'm flamboyant . . . even eccentric, but I think I'm just as normal as anybody to a certain extent, except that I have the resources to do some of these crazy things."

Resources are in so many cases the key which opens the door to the reputation for bizarre conduct. Caruth Byrd's oil, films, real estate and cattle have made him worth more than $100 million. Described as America's most wacky millionaire, he owns two dozen cars and trucks, a bus converted into a home on wheels, seven houses and a German Messerschmidt fighter plane.

His chief distraction from business is his big appetite for practical jokes. These reportedly run from wiring up the ladies' toilets to administer mild shocks, to putting dead fish into the hubcaps of cars, and serving rubber eggs to his guests at mealtimes. At night he runs a musical group consisting of his own executives. "My attorney plays the clarinet; the head of my farming operations plays left-handed guitar and sings; my drummer is president of my corporation. I play piano and organ; and my bodyguard plays the spoons." It's only a guess that his accountant is adept at fiddling!

His one ambition for a time was to meet the legendary monster, Bigfoot, to put him on a plane and have a drink with him on the way back home. He donated $5,000 towards an expedition to track the monster down.

"But I never found him."

Another rich Texan sent for his tailor who lived in Chicago, to fly to Fort Worth to fit one of his horses with a mink suit. He had already bought several for himself from the same tailor. The coats and trouser cuffs were specially cut to display an array of diamonds.

Naturally, he directed that his horse's mink suit should also have cut-away turn-ups to show off its diamond-set hooves.

Captain Sticky

A magnificent shiny black Lincoln drew up outside the high-class restaurant. A standard fluttered above it, and on it was the sign CAUTION—CAPED CRUSADER ON DUTY.

Out of it stepped a fantastic figure in crushed velvet trousers, with blue brocade blouse. Swinging a gold cane, he entered the restaurant. Since it was Hollywood, the staff showed little surprise and only a few of the guests turned to look. One was a famous film star who rose and stood facing the newcomer.

"Howdy, I'm John Wayne."

"Sir," replied the fantastic figure. "I'm Captain Sticky, Supreme Commander-in-Chief in the war against evil."

"Well, Captain," drawled Wayne, "there sure ought to be a place in the world for a fella like you."

The redoubtable Captain Sticky was otherwise known as Richard Festa, a Californian glass-fibre tycoon who would occasionally leave his business to change character. In the daytime he would don his blue catsuit, gold boots, flying helmet and gold cape and ride off in his "Stickmobile"—often with a police escort! Captain Sticky had the money to act out his fantasies of ridding the world of evil.

Not that encounters with him were always plain sailing. One woman had just seen the film *The Exorcist.* When she came out of the cinema and saw on his car the sign THE EYES OF THE DEVIL ARE NEVER BLINDED she thought Satan had really arrived and hurriedly called the police.

Captain Sticky's great dream is to build an empire—the World Organization Against Evil. "But," he said, "if the whole thing were to collapse right now, it would have been a fantastic experience. I have no regrets."

The Australian Joker

On April 1st, 1978, Mr. Dick Smith of Sydney, Australia, an electronics millionaire, decided to play a first-class April Fool's Day prank on the rest of the community. The idea was to bring a giant iceberg into the port.

In the morning, in sight of thousands of astonished onlookers, the "iceberg" was towed in. On it was a radio reporter broadcasting the latest news of the operation. When they heard it, listeners and reporters flocked to the vicinity of the port, and scores of small craft raced in to inspect the unusual object. Ferries were held up as their skippers politely got out of the way.

In his broadcast Mr. Smith told the public that he intended to moor the iceberg near the Opera House. There it would be cut up into tiny cubes—"Dicksicles" he called them—and sold for ten cents each.

It couldn't be done. The "iceberg" was an imitation, a barge covered with white plastic sheeting and fire-fighting foam. In the gloom and drizzle of the early April dawn it had looked just like the real thing.

Mr. Smith got his laugh and nobody was particularly disappointed. "The prank cost me $1,450," he said. "I do these things for kicks. It takes the boredom out of everyday work."

THE ENGLISH ECCENTRICS

A Singular Breed

It is probably true that England has brought forth more truly bizarre characters than any other country in the world though it must be admitted that the United States is rapidly catching up.

The reason for this is rooted in history. Society in England developed in such a way that, from the 16th century at least, there were three social classes—nobility, gentry and commoners—that were not exclusive and never lost touch with each other. In this nursery of democracy lords-lieutenants, sheriffs of counties and justices of the peace mingled freely with the parsons, churchwardens and other voluntary officers of many a self-governing parish as well as with every Tom, Dick and Harry who ploughed their fields, took in their harvests and shod their horses.

The squire or the nobleman was a public figure, the outstanding example in literature being Addison's Sir Roger de Coverley who went to church, took part in the same services as his tenants, bawled at them should they dare to snore during the sermon but never begrudged himself a nap. And nobody thought a whit the worse of him for it. How dared they anyway? With all his shortcomings he was a cultured, kind and caring landlord who did what he could in the interests of all those whose well-being depended on him.

Moreover, since he was a public figure, if he had any eccentricities or unusual traits of character they were readily noticed, understood, appreciated and, on the whole, recorded. Few of the squires did any great harm to anybody except themselves—even if in some cases their conduct verged on lunacy.

The antics of some of them, however, had they been poor people, would have landed them either in the parish lock-up, the county gaol or the madhouse.

Which brings us to one important point. The bizarre personality in Old England usually had something to be bizarre on—to wit, money. Hence the eccentrics of Old England were in the main titled gentry, squires, self-made industrialists and in some cases learned gentlemen and parsons who for the most part possessed some of this wealth so essential to an independent life. Under these conditions the country, at least from the 16th century onwards, produced literally thousands of these bizarre characters. Their exploits kept the publishers and printers of the day in business, so plentiful were the books, pamphlets and broadside sheets relating to them.

The Mad Aristocracy

Lord North, when Prime Minister of England, was once sitting on the Government bench listening with eyes closed to a member of the opposition making a long and extremely boring speech.

"—— and I must observe, that though the matter on which I am speaking is of vital importance to the well-being of this Kingdom, my noble lord is now fast asleep!"

Lord North slowly opened one eye. "I wish to God I was," he observed.

In those days a young aristocrat, if he was to command any respect from his fellows at all, had not only to possess wit, he had to have *bottom*. This word is not used today in the sense it was some 150 years ago, but it signified a unique combination of pluck, doggedness, courage, endurance, devil-may-care spirit, flamboyance and arrogance.

Of these traits the supreme example of his day was Jack Mytton, the Mad Squire of Halston. He must have had the constitution of an ox to have stood up to the ordeals to which he subjected his body. Every morning he drank four bottles of port, varying this with eau-de-Cologne and even quicksilver when his supplies ran low. He was accustomed to test his physique by regularly jumping over the park railings, and to test his nerves by driving in his chaise at maximum speed on narrow twisting country roads in the dead of night. He could not bear to be unsure of anything. So when friends wondered if it was possible to ride a horse over a rabbit warren—he did. Nor was he surprised when the horse threw him and he broke an arm.

After a day's hunting he considered it natural to take his horse Baronet into the library to share with him a bottle or two of port. On occasion the squire was invited to dinner. He made a memorable entrance riding on the back of a brown bear which bit him in the leg when he used the spurs on it. He was not often asked out!

He also kept 60 cats and 2,000 (two thousand!) dogs which he fed on champagne and beefsteak. One day, to cure an attack of hiccoughs by giving himself a shock, he deliberately set fire to his shirt. He received the shock he wanted but died of his burns, and his last words were, "Well, the hiccup has gone, by God!"

Another of the same breed was Jemmy Hirst, a Yorkshire landowner and follower of the hunt, who sometimes went after the fox mounted on the back of a large black bull with a pack of young pigs instead of hounds.

Squire Waterton, much more learned but no less foolhardy than Mytton or Hirst, liked to hang upside down in trees and is reputed to have said while scratching his head with his big toe, "I don't know why people think I'm eccentric."

Possibly it may have had something to do with the fact that the squire kept crocodiles in his pond.

Borderline Cases

The bizarre was common enough but much less frequently recorded among the trading and lower classes and their object, more than anything else, was to attract attention. Every tradesman knows that if you can make people notice you your sales will go up.

One of the shopkeepers at the turn of the 19th century was Nathaniel Bentley who kept a warehouse in Leadenhall Street,

London. He refused to wash himself or ever to clean up his premises. "It's of no use, sir," he would say. "If I wash my hands today they'll only be dirty again tomorrow."

The following lines were written to him:

"O say, thou enemy of soap and towels!
Hast no compassion lurking in thy bowels?
Think what the neighbours suffer by thy whim
Of keeping self and home in such a trim!"

It made no difference. He maintained that even to clean his shop front would so alter its appearance as to ruin his trade.

Bentley was only one of the many salesmen who attracted trade through bizarre dress and conduct. James Sharpe Egland, better known as the Flying Pieman, cooked his wares in Spa Fields, sprinted with his basket through Old London selling his hot pies on the run and keeping up a ceaseless torrent of entertaining chatter. His friend, Martin van Butchell, sold medicines and gingerbreads in Hyde Park, and painted his pony in bright hues including red and blue and always carried the jawbone of an ass. Between times he published philosophical pamphlets that nobody could understand.

There is, of course, a stage where oddity merges into insanity and such cases can only be pitied. On the verge was Daniel Dancer of Harrow, London, who was accustomed to wash himself in sand to save soap and water and never to change his clothes or sheets. His horse was allowed only two shoes, the four feet taking turns to be shod.

The Gastronomic Doctor

In 1850 the price of whalebone in England was £150 per ton, then within a few months owing to the introduction of crinoline for women's clothing it suddenly rocketed to a fantastic £650. Nobody regretted this more than Dr. Francis Buckland, not because of the distress caused to the fashionable ladies of the day but because of its effects on the whale.

Francis Trevelyan Buckland (1826–1880) was one of Britain's most distinguished zoologists. Like Darwin, he had an absorbing interest in anything that lived. Even when a student at

Oxford he had his own private menagerie which included a tame bear.

At a time when few people were thinking seriously about the nation's food resources, Buckland was already pressing for the need to increase meat supplies by introducing new animals such as bison, kangaroos, even ostriches into the country. He was almost a century before his time when he advocated putting a stop to the destruction of the spawn and fry of sea fish by the too extensive use of trawls.

His enthusiasm led him into what seemed the most eccentric ways. He recognized that eating was largely conditioned by the habits of a people. Some of the dishes Chinese or even continental friends relished were enough to turn the stomach of the fastidious English. If this was so, then English eating habits had to be radically altered if only in the interests of national survival.

In 1862 Buckland was responsible for the annual dinner of the Society for the Acclimatisation of Animals in the United Kingdom. On his menu were kangaroo meat from Australia and South-East Asia Tripang sea-slug. The guests managed the first but no more than a few were able even to sample the second.

In his private regimen Buckland enjoyed a variety rarely achieved by others. He was specially fond of rhinoceros pie, boiled elephant's trunk, and mouse on toast, the last of which he served to his fellow-students at Oxford. He suggested that slug soup and garden snails could be made both to look and taste appetizing. Occasionally he served to his guests such delicacies as roast or boiled dog, tortoise, pickled horse or potted ostrich. His wife joined him in appreciating roast ostrich which she described as tasting very much like coarse turkey. It gave his friend Sir Richard Owen a severe attack of indigestion.

Quite apart from the fact that such a diet must have raised his living costs considerably, he was probably faced by polite refusals to join his dinner parties.

Though Buckland considered it his duty to sample anything which might serve as an article of diet, there were some dishes which even he found difficult. Broiled porpoise head he described as tasting like the wick of an oil lamp. It was a pity, he said, that earwigs were so bitter. Stewed mole and bluebottles he found to be beyond even his own wide-ranging taste.

During a meal with friends one day the conversation turned towards the subject of unconventional dishes, and Buckland confided to his friends that he had never yet eaten the heart of a king. One of his friends happened to be in possession of the heart of Louis XIV of France (died 1715) which had been plundered from the royal tomb at the time of the Revolution. After more than a century it had shrivelled to the size of a prune. During the meal it was handed round to the members of the party in turn. Buckland popped it into his mouth and swallowed it.

"God Is a Gentleman"

The English gentleman in the 19th century believed himself to be the salt of the earth. Whatever anybody else thought, he had the immoveable conviction that he was right. Consequently, once when the Victorian diarist Augustus Hare read morning prayers to his household he never mentioned the name of God, for "God," he explained, "is undoubtedly a gentleman and no gentleman cares to be praised to his face."

Lord Berners, the fourteenth of the line, when travelling first class by rail would go to any extremes to keep others out of the compartment he was occupying. While the train was standing at the station he would lean out of the open window wearing dark glasses, and with a maniacal grin on his face, invite all who passed by to come in. They usually didn't but if his first defense crumpled and they took their seats, he would go on playing the madman, shuffling about, taking his temperature every four or five minutes and reading his newspaper upside down. Most of them soon got out again.

Lord Berners was no lunatic. He installed an organ in the back of his limousine, for he was a musician and composer as well as a passable artist and novelist.

But he was a person of rank, which made all the difference. Moreover he was no snob—unlike the Duke of Wellington who was a passionate enemy of the railways because, as he put it, "They encourage the lower classes to travel!"

There are few, if any, of the old breed left although Major Graham of Claverhouse must qualify—he was brave and eccentric to a point. His son recalls: "He was a professional soldier, a bit of an anachronism I suppose. He insisted on landing on the beaches of Dunkirk armed with nothing but a crossbow. The first German who appeared he transfixed neatly through the navel with his arrow. He was sent for by his commanding officer and expected to be given some tremendous award for gallantry; in fact he was banished from the front and sent back to be a policeman in Piccadilly."

The Last of the Great Eccentrics

The bizarre today, if it exists at all, exists in very inhospitable soil for, taxation being what it is, eccentricity among once-wealthy families is being choked at its source.

But not entirely. Until recently the village of West Dean in Sussex, an estate composed of eleven farms and 2,000 acres of woodland, belonged to a man named Edward James. He is the son of Willie James, an American multi-millionaire, and a well-known Edwardian hostess. The youngest child and only son of his parents, Edward lost his father at the age of five, was handed over to a nurse and rarely saw his socialite mother. He tells how one Sunday before going to church his mother called to the nurse to bring one of the children to accompany her and on being asked which one replied, "Oh, the one that best matches my blue dress."

The emotional deprivation of his childhood did much to fashion the fabric of his later life.

"I have been a surrealist from birth, not from intention," he says. "When I was a child I had the most extraordinary surrealist fantasies." These arose from his having to rest at times when he was wide-awake and longing to get out into the fresh air. He describes how in the morning when at seven o'clock he wanted to be up and away, he was forced to lie in bed until nurse came in at half-past eight. During that time he invented a world of his own. His bedclothes became a flying city, his pillows domes and he, in his palace, floated in imagination high above the world.

At Oxford James was able to flaunt his wealth, to drive his own Rolls-Royce and to pilot his own plane. His rooms were lined in purple and gold. Here he followed up his interest in the arts, made friends with John, now Sir John, Betjeman, and several other rising poets and artists.

At the age of twenty-four James married Tilly Losch, a popular actress and dancer with whom he had fallen madly in love. Unfortunately the marriage turned out a complete failure, and she left him. Whereupon he embarked on the most expensive scheme to win her back, even going as far as to finance an entire season of ballet in Paris in which she starred, hiring the best company and bringing Brecht and Kurt Weill from Germany to write the libretto and music of an operetta for her. But it was all to no avail and disillusioned he left for America.

For a period he lived among the intellectuals in Hollywood, including Aldous Huxley and Christopher Isherwood, but after a quarrel with one of the group, he went to Mexico. He has lived there ever since, having found, some 400 miles north of Mexico City, a deserted site among beautiful scenery. He adopted a Mexican family and there he built a smallish house without even a bathroom. He resolved to make the place into another Garden of Eden and spent years importing and preserving wild life, bringing animals and birds from all parts of the world to settle on the estate.

After a freak snowstorm he resolved to build a new house, more splendid than had ever been seen in the area, and which no kind of weather could harm. Spurred on by the shapes of the trees in the forest, the rocks and James' own surrealist visions, the work was begun in 1962 and has continued ever since, 30 workmen being employed continuously at a cost of some thousand dollars a week. Here, like Kubla Khan, he plans and creates the towers and walls of his pleasure-dome, with its arches and leaf-shaped pillars, a house for his immense collection of surrealist art.

In 1964 he gave away the family home at West Dean for it to be set up as a college devoted to the preservation and teaching of ancient crafts.

We have come a long way from the days of the hard-hunting, hard-drinking old English squire.

Looking to the Future

In 1964, John Goodman brought forth a brilliant idea. The 20th century was rapidly approaching its fourth quarter, and he believed it was time to make preparations for the coming of the 21st.

So he began his own campaign. The idea was to get the leaders of every municipality in the world to state openly the faith that the earth would survive into the next century, and to give practical shape to that faith in deeds.

From his bachelor home in Golders Green, London, he set to work searching out the names of mayors and heads of government throughout the world to whom at his own expense he sent circular letters outlining his plan. Among the suggestions he made were schemes for planting trees, a number of trade fairs in various countries, and a huge central celebration to be held on an artificial island complex in mid-Atlantic at 27 degrees N by 40 degrees W—roughly halfway between the Bahamas and the Canaries. The celebration was to be open to anybody in the world able to visit it.

"To me," he said, "the very thought of the year 2000 produces shivers of excitement. Just to get there would be a wonderful achievement, but to celebrate it—that will be the best party the world has ever seen."

Out of the 50,000 letters he sent out, no replies were received from 45,000; a few replied that they were sorry they would be unable to accept the invitation to participate, and 187 expressed approval and interest. So he founded the World Association for Celebrating the Year 2000—WACY for short.

Lack of response did not deter him. The *Anchorage Daily News*, Alaska, reported that Mayor George M. Sullivan had been appointed President, and in England there was a large number of individual members.

"For ten years," said John Goodman in 1974, "I have lived this dream and if God gives me health I shall see it through until the year 2000. If I offered the governments of the world an atom bomb they would probably take it. Instead I am offering a chance of world peace and happiness and people turn me down. Something must be wrong."

The newspaper report ends: "When you meet a man like John Goodman you wonder if it is the world that is WACY, not him."

The Distaff Side

"My mother," said Lord Francis Williams, "a charming and somewhat eccentric lady, had a deep belief that to go to a public library was decidedly immoral, so highly dangerous that she would seize my library books and put them in the oven in the belief that they must be covered with germs and that the best way to deal with them was by roasting them."

Over the ages women have not had the same latitude for the expression of the bizarre as men.

The lady of the following story is a delightful exception. At Epsom, the English racecourse famous for the Derby, a one-day course for officials was in progress. The conference was debating the question of the gypsies, who always frequented the track and whom many considered a nuisance. In the middle of the discussion a small stoutish woman in a peaked cap and with a scarf wound round her head under it, burst into the conference room and, speaking in a deep voice with careful emphasis, said:

"I have heard of your decision to bar the gypsies. I applaud it, and I trust you will applaud mine. You will now have neither paddock nor grandstand." With that she swept out of the conference room.

"Who on earth was that?" asked someone.

"That, my dear fellow, was Lady Sybil Grant. She owns both the paddock *and* the grandstand."

The decision to ban the gypsies was reversed, and gypsies have frequented the racecourse ever since.

Lady Sybil was the best-known woman eccentric in modern Britain. In 1949, detectives were detailed to guard her horse that was fancied for a possible place in the next race. They asked her if there was someplace where one could sleep.

"What?" exclaimed Lady Sybil. "You can't fool me. I've read my Peter Cheyney and I know detectives *never* sleep." With that she departed.

Lady Sybil was also something of a fresh-air fiend. When she travelled by train she took a long tube and, clipping one end to the window, she would hold the other to her nose. Halfway down the tube was an ozone pad. Everything would go well until she offered the tube to a fellow-passenger who, knowing who she was, refused to try it. The result was bound to be a disaster for, through the moving of the pad he would get, instead of ozone, a stream of smut in his face.

Her own private bus had no windscreen, as it had been removed to allow free passage of air, to the great discomfiture of her chauffeur and passengers.

She took a great dislike to sleeping away from home, and when she was forced to do so, insisted on sleeping in her own bus in the driveway. At her house in Shropshire, one of the three she possessed, she often slept on a platform up a tree.

The gentlemen's lavatory in one of her three houses was papered entirely with rejection slips from editors of magazines to which she had sent poems and articles. The only poem of hers which is believed to be extant is one she said she had used whenever she wished to leave a dull dinner party. It read:

"The meat is tough
And so am I.
I've had enough,
And so, goodbye."

Lady Sybil also painted animals, which she loved. To be candid she painted rather poorly but, ever the enthusiast, she judged that the public would like the subjects of her paintings rather more than the quality. She got a hawker's license from the London County Council and when Cruft's Dog Show came along, she sat on the pavement outside the hall showing her paintings to passers-by.

She never lost her great interest in the welfare of gypsies and instead of staying at hotels when she was travelling, she would have the driver of her bus make for the nearest gypsy encampment where she knew she would be among friends.

Lady Sybil died in 1955 in her mid-seventies.

THE LONERS

Love and War

There are times when every one of us wants to get away from it all. Edward James did it and it cost him several fortunes. So did Howard Hughes with vastly different results. His life and the motives behind his self-imposed and miserable isolation have long been the subjects of comment and hardly need be repeated.

What makes such people retire into solitude? Sometimes the reason is personal. Lawrence Say, a bearded hermit, died in 1977 at the early age of 45 after having lived in a cave near Bath, England, for 25 years. He had once been a smart young man, one of the best-dressed in the city, and became a hermit after having been jilted by his girl friend. No persuasion could make him return home.

Other hermits are driven to solitude through contemplating the sorry state of the world. Kei Agatsuma, a Japanese woman, lived in caves and bush huts on Stewart Island, New Zealand. She was found and convicted in Invercargill for overstaying her visitor's permit because, as she put it, she dreaded returning to

Tokyo, "that jungle of subways, cars, concrete blocks and tall buildings." Who's to say *she* is the odd one?

Silvano Franchi also decided that he did not like the way the world was shaping up. It was 1935 and at that time Mussolini and Hitler were making ominous signs of coming war. Franchi, then a 25-year-old bachelor, decided that he would do something about it and shut out the world completely, retiring to a tiny stone cottage at Falcinello on the coast north of Rome. Since then nobody has seen him. When his military call-up papers arrived the local doctor and the mayor sent them back with the comment "unfit to serve—he is mad."

Since the day of his disappearance his sister took his meals daily to the hut, and collected the dishes from the previous day together with the wickerwork baskets he had made to be sold in the local market. The villagers called him *il Tasso*—the badger—because he came out only by night to tend his little garden, his eyes having become accustomed to the dark through living so long in the dim interior of the hut.

A happier recluse was Bill Johnson who lived in a forest fastness less than a mile from the busy Kingston–Leatherhead road in Surrey. A London docker at the age of 47 in 1933, he had decided that he had had enough of industrial unrest and the eternal squabbling between one side and the other. "One day," he said, "I decided that I couldn't take any more. I had just seen a man beaten at the dock gates and I didn't want to see it happen again." He made up his mind to make a clean break.

He had no wife, no ties and a few pounds saved up. He bought a bicycle, a World War I army tent, a kettle, two pans, an axe and a modest stock of provisions and set up house in dense woods on common land near Leatherhead.

The years went by peacefully. Once a week he cycled to town to buy provisions. He knew from local conversation that there was war between Great Britain and Germany. When old enough he drew his weekly pension, the greater part of which he saved in the Post Office. He was amiable and did no harm to anybody. The police left him alone and he remained in his hide-out for more than 40 years.

The Prisoners

On the 18th of March, 1952, a broken-down figure apparently on the verge of suicide knocked at the door of a French widow and her daughter at Freville near Cherbourg, pleading for help. His name, he said, was Auguste Pouppeville, and he had spent most of the war period in German prison camps.

The widow and her daughter took pity on him. They took him into their home and for 20 years he was never seen by any other persons. His bed-sitting room was a windowless cupboard in which a bed, a candle and two cardboard boxes were all the furniture. The walls were papered with old newspapers, the ceiling was made from sheets cut from the sides of cardboard boxes. His rations were bread, fruit and a gallon of diluted wine a week. By day he would help the two women in the two-roomed cottage, but when anybody knocked at the door he scuttled away into his cupboard and locked the door. Through lack of exercise the muscles of his legs atrophied and he walked with difficulty.

But he was happy and yet fearful lest knowledge of his presence would start a village scandal and destroy his hard-won security.

The story, unlike others of the same kind, seems to have had a happy ending. In 1972 the widow died of cancer. Sympathetic neighbours called on the daughter to see if they could give any help. One of them by chance opened the cupboard and found—A MAN!

The whole village was in a flutter. What had Marie and her mother been up to? But Marie stood her ground. Before her mother died she had called on Auguste and made him promise never to leave her daughter.

"——so now we're getting married."

"Yes," said Auguste. "I can come out now, but I can't take a job; my legs aren't strong enough. Still, I can earn a little money by catching a few eels."

Eighty-Four Years a Hermit

The strangest story of all is that of Bozo Kucik, reputed to have been a hundred years old in 1972.

One autumn day in 1888 he was landed by his father on a desert island off the Incoronata Archipelago near the Dalmatian coast at Fiume (now Rijeka) and was left to fend for himself. He was only 16 when his father took him there, kissed him goodbye and said, "I hope all goes well with you, my son." Then he walked back to the little sailing boat and set off back to his home port of Zadar.

There was a reason for the father's strange conduct. He was a poor peasant, a widower with seven growing children he could not afford to feed, so he called his sons together and asked each of them to decide his own future. The Robinson Crusoe existence was Bozo's own choice.

In the early days his father brought him small presents, sometimes a little food, sometimes an article of threadbare clothing, a knife, a tin cup, a cooking pot or a towel. But the journey was long. In time the visits ceased and Bozo lived from one year's end to the next without seeing or speaking to another human being. In the meantime there were two world wars. His island had been first Austrian, then Italian in 1919, then after the second war part of Yugoslavia, and he did not know a thing about it.

He lived on and on until in 1972 his island was visited by a crew of fishermen. They found him near naked with little more clothing than a string of rabbit skins round his neck linked together with strips of a type of rattan palm-straw. By shouting from a distance of about 20 yards they managed to make out the meaning of what he said in the simple Bosnian dialect of his youth. He would not let them inspect his home, a windowless stone hut, and if they tried to approach him he either threatened them with a rock in each hand or made as if to run away.

They talked with him for two hours. He knew nothing of war and could not understand why any man should want to kill another except to eat him as one does a rabbit. When asked how old he was he answered, "about a hundred years."

They left him a bottle of beer, some second-hand clothing and tins of canned food, showing him from a distance how to open them. Then, after wishing him a happy hundredth birthday, they put out to sea.

There have been Robinson Crusoes galore and more than one recent discovery of a Japanese soldier on a deserted island who knew nothing about the conclusion of peace more than 30 years ago. But there has been hardly anything to equal the story of Bozo's 84 years of solitude.

Collectors and Hoarders

There is a big difference between the collector and the hoarder. The collector is choosy; he goes for the best, throws out or sells the inferior. He cherishes what he has gathered together, classifies, arranges, catalogues and produces a choice accumulation, whether it be large or small, of which anyone would be proud.

A hoarder, on the other hand, amasses quantity rather than quality. He is the human magpie, filling his nest with anything that takes his fancy. He has no sense of order and lets articles lie around or pile up anywhere, dirty, among rubbish, gathering dust and of use to nobody but himself. Apart from the odd article here and there, the hoarder has generally little idea where anything he possesses can be found.

Such a one was Clarence A. Browne of Long Island, New York. His once lovely 14-room house in this high-income community became an eyesore during the five years he lived in it, without heat, water or electricity. The litter inside the house—newspapers, empty soda bottles, blankets and sweaters—reached two to three feet in thickness so that he had to climb over it like a mountain goat.

The heater was broken. The pipes had burst and had not been repaired. There was water damage before the water was turned off because of non-payment of bills. The doors and door-jambs became loose because of the constant beatings they took when he forced the doors open against litter which slid back against them once they were closed again.

The result was that at the age of 51 he faced eviction from the only home he had ever known. This left him with one overriding problem: what was to happen to his collection of 750,000 records including every one made by George Gershwin, the only record Lupe Velez made on the original Zonophone label, "Two White Hands" sung by Adolphe Menjou in mint condition, and many others.

There were records everywhere—in piles on the floor, in the refrigerator, on tables, on the fireplace mantel, in cartons, ranging from old shellacs and laminated discs to the post-war LP's of polyvinyl chloride.

In one respect Browne seemed to differ from all other hoarders for he apparently had information about all the records stored in his head. Ask him about "In the Garden," for instance, and he would reply, "It was written by C. Austin Mills for the Billy Sunday evangelist crusade of 1916. Papa loved it."

Papa was a relatively wealthy man, an executive with the Cadillac Division of General Motors who died in 1970 leaving his son $120,000 of which $48,000 was given as the value of the house, already slipping into disrepair. The rest, he said, he had given away to friends, $40,000 to a bus driver who said he needed it to set himself up in business in a bar. "I can't refuse anybody," he mused ruefully. "At least I didn't spend it on women and song."

If what he said was true, he had certainly had too many fair-weather friends, for when the money ran out he found that those he had helped stopped speaking to him and turned the other way.

He finished up on welfare, his house lost for failing payment of taxes. The value in his property remained entirely in his records.

If only Clarence the Hoarder had been Clarence the Collector!

Hoarders are often also recluses, for hiding and hoarding tend to go together. This happened in the case of David Mason who died at the age of 77 in his house in Worthing, England.

Only after his death did officials and relatives discover what had kept him so busy in life. He was a compulsive hoarder who could never resist the special advertising offers he saw in magazines and newspapers. Day after day he took out his cheque book and sent off for silver medallions, the collected works of famous authors, long-playing records, reproductions of well-known paintings, replicas of old clocks and anything else that caught his eye. He was too busy searching for new offers even to open some of the packages that he had received.

His house was chock-full of thousands of assorted objects. In one room alone there were more than 100 pieces of camera equipment. Others were stacked with sports gear, carved chessmen, and model railways. Not a corner of the house was left empty. He had everything needed for fishing except the water, sailing except the boat, skiing except the snow, shooting except the butts, and archery except the targets. Three old rifles were found in his grandfather clock. Gold coins were strewn all over the floor of his garage, in the kitchen and even in the oven.

Like Clarence of Long Island he had been left an enormous amount of money by his father and had never had to work in his life. Like Clarence he had lived alone, his marriage having broken up in 1930. Unlike Clarence he had held on to much of his fortune and when he died he left something in excess of £200,000. The auction of his goods raised one tenth of that sum.

There is nothing bizarre in being a collector but some collectors go in for strange things. Sam Brooks is a retired postman who spends his time travelling the roads of the United States by bus carrying a sack full of newspaper clippings. And every clipping has his name on it in print.

For Sam is a newspaper clipping collector who calls at the offices of newspapers all over the States trying to get his name into them. He noses out reporters from Brooklyn to Chicago, from Chicago to Houston, Houston to Atlanta and back to Brooklyn again with the request:

"Please put my name in your paper!"

Sometimes he is just tolerated, sometimes put off, often he makes people feel sorry for him—enough for them to do what he asks. In some places security guards are given orders to throw him out as soon as he is spotted.

But he perseveres. After a hundred successes even Sam begins to be news. Last time he was heard of, and that is a while ago now, his score was 149.

Not a bad record, and harmless enough. But no good for the Guinness Book, for he couldn't hold a candle to Frank Sinatra.

ARE THEY A DYING BREED?

Eccentricity is a quality which is becoming more and more prized in our over-ordered society. It may be impracticable, uncomfortable, at times a nuisance. But it denotes character and individuality. It also pleases the escapist imp in all of us. That's why we like to read about crackpots.

"But," says John Stuart Mill, it "has always abounded when and where strength of character has abounded; and the amount of eccentricity in a society has always been proportioned to the amount of genius, mental vigour and moral courage it contained."

How then do we stand today when bureaucracy is growing, taxation is high and government interferes in almost every walk of life? Where are we to look for those people whose bizarre traits we are said to prize so highly? "The times are against us I fear," wrote the humorist Jonathan Routh. "The taxman has ensured that there are fewer rich in our midst who can afford to indulge in mere whims."

But is it altogether true that we need rich people to produce bizarre characters? True, there are not as many being ridiculous in the grand style as there were a century ago, though there are exceptions.

For some, however, the bizarre adds another dimension to character and is deliberately put on like a garment, for it adds notoriety. And some people, like Dali, have the faculty of reducing it to a fine art.

There are too, as we have seen, those who can rise above anything the taxman can do to them. But besides these there are thousands upon thousands, some loners, some in groups, who are up to the most extraordinary antics.

Art under the Sea

Bob van Kay is an uncommon sort of artist. For his work he needs a boat, an oxygen tank and flippers. His underwater studio is a couple of miles off shore at a spot on the Gulf of Mexico. He dons his scuba-diving gear, grabs his art materials, rolls overboard and swims 25 to 35 feet to the bottom. There he sets up shop for an average of 45 minutes at a time, lying on his stomach, steadying the palette with his left hand and dabbing the brush with his right. He has some difficulty in getting the paint to adhere to the canvas, and progress is much slower than in the conventional way of painting, but he thinks the results so far have been worthwhile. He has just finished a picture of a woman scuba diver gliding over a reef and picking up a shell, done on a 22 × 28 inch canvas using regular commercial oil paints in shades of blue and white.

"Oddballs of the World, Unite!"

From England

The Reverend Colin Cooper of Gorleston made a promise to his congregation that for once he would keep his mouth shut. But they got his sermons all the same for he brought a ventriloquist's doll into the pulpit and within a very short time he had doubled his congregation. He still uses it—the vicar is no dummy!

In 1948, an Oxfordshire man tried to cure his baldness by putting a poultice of warm cowdung on his head. In fact, being soft and engendering heat, cowdung has been used of old for tumors, for drawing boils and for placing on the chest and back in cases of pneumonia. Unfortunately it didn't grow hair. Other men have tried rotted mushrooms and I myself have known men to rub paraffin or kerosene in.

Ernest Digwood in 1977 gave his lawyers a shock. He died

leaving his money—£26,000—"to the Lord, when He returns to earth." But Ernest, a canny individual, added that the Lord "must offer proof of His identity." If in the year 2057 he has not appeared the money is to go to the reigning monarch of England.

Mrs. Alice Gilbert was retiring from her post as lavatory attendant at St. Paul's Cray in Kent, and everybody wanted to wish her well, so Alice, known to regulars as Mrs. Loo, handed round drinks, sandwiches and cake on her last day in office. The proceedings, which naturally took place in the lavatories, ended with everybody singing:

"Goodbye, Mrs. Loo.
We're sorry to be leaving you,
Boo-hoo!"

Then all the ladies retired to the cubicles and gave one concerted flush to all the toilets.

From Italy

Alfred Pallini, a bookbinder of Terni, Umbria, had a call one day from a mysterious stranger who wanted 100 pages bound into a book. Each page turned out to be a 10,000 lire banknote, and the customer paid another 10,000 for the binding. Time after time he returned, always with the same order until fifty similar books of notes had been bound, all bearing on the cover the same inscription in French—MONEY HAS NO COLOUR. Four months later the stranger entered again and ordered the 51st volume, making a total of more than £36,000 ($72,000).

He never came back for it.

From Indonesia

Two gentlemen, Mr. Djambi and Mr. Hasnuddin of Haruku both claimed the same sago tree as his property. They decided to settle the dispute in the traditional way, by seeing who could remain under water longest. Watched by all the villagers they weighted themselves with stones and jumped into the sea.

They were both drowned.

From India

Two Sikh factions were feuding and had met, sword in hand,

to fight it out. A social worker, foreseeing tragedy, bargained with them and finally persuaded them to settle their differences peacefully. But tradition dictated that blood must be spilled.

So the blood bank was sent for and every man gave a pint.

From the United States

Herbert Dengler, a teacher of Minneapolis, is not satisfied with his name. He wants to be called Mr. One Zero Six Nine (1069) which, he says, symbolizes his interrelationship with society and his personal and philosophical identity since every digit has significance for him. Judge Donald Barbeau rejected the request on the grounds that the imposition of numbers upon people, while being a necessary accommodation to computers . . . is nevertheless an offence to basic human dignity and is inherently totalitarian.

Stan Cohen of Hollywood provided for the barmitzvah of his son Harvey with a magnificent party at the Orange Bowl in Miami, with waitresses dressed as cheerleaders and bartenders as referees. He sent invitations in the form of football tickets, had a party tent erected at the 50-yard line, and hired a 100-member high school marching band to provide the music. "I never expected anything like this," said his son.

Mrs. Josie Holton issued an edition of 100 copies of *The Rime of the Ancient Mariner* costing $200 each. They were printed on seven varieties of seaweed. "This is my first attempt to produce a book printed on seaweed," said Mrs. Holton. "I used edible seaweeds only. If you get fed up with the book you can always eat it." Kelp!

Well, How Daffy Can You Get?

Miss Ruth van Herpen once visited the Oxford Museum of Modern Art where she saw a picture which moved her tremendously, so much so that she walked up to it and kissed it. When approached by a museum official she said she was so sorry for the picture. "I only kissed it to cheer it up; it looked so cold." A museum official ruefully estimated it might cost £700 ($1,400) to clean the lipstick off the £10,000 ($20,000) painting which had been loaned to the Museum by a New York gallery.

A Zero Card has been produced by a company in Great Missenden, England, bearing the picture of former Prime Minister Henry Addington on the front as a token of its uselessness. Costing $2.00, it is guaranteed good for absolutely nothing. The Company claim that they have developed a revolutionary new economic theory of "live now—pay now."

General Sherman, the Federal hero of the American Civil War, was once the special guest at a banquet that was followed by a reception. Among the people who shook hands with him was a man whose face seemed familiar but whom he could not place.

"Who are you?" the General asked in a whisper as he welcomed the guest.

The man's face flushed as he answered, "Made your shirts, sir."

"Ah, of course," exclaimed the General. Then, turning to the receiving committee he said: "Gentlemen, allow me to present my dear friend Major Shurtz."

Where Does It Stop?

The borderline between bizarre conduct and mental disorder is very ill-defined so that it is sometimes difficult to distinguish one from the other. There are true stories of the London bank clerk who used to encase his head when he went to bed at night by wrapping aluminium foil round it because he believed the police car radio messages would otherwise turn him into a criminal while he slept; the Bradford man who wore his shoes on the wrong feet and turned his trousers back to front to confuse disease-bearing germs; and the woman who used always to carry an open umbrella, even sleeping with it open over her head in bed because she thought it prevented people spreading the story that she was a woman of loose morals.

One thing is certain—we treated the mentally abnormal with more sympathy in times gone by, not as outcasts to be shut away, but merely as different. Many a village halfwit was once regarded merely as a "wee bit eccentric" and, when he indulged in bizarre imaginings the rest of the community went with him, joined in his fantasies and thus got the best out of him.

Thus Oliver, who was in his prime in an English village some 60 to 70 years ago, was just such a person. Every Sunday at chapel he was to be seen in his place in one corner of the gallery. He couldn't read and often used to stand during hymn-singing with his book upside down loudly mouthing unintelligible sounds. He talked to Jesus Christ as a friend. Everybody accepted him; ridicule was just not tolerated.

He was a roadsweeper weekdays. His wages were £1 a week which he insisted on having in a single gold sovereign—no more, no less. When the roadsweepers' wages were raised by a shilling he refused to take it, and it had to be given him by some subterfuge or other. During the 1914-18 war when golden sovereigns were replaced by the £1 note he was disconsolate for weeks.

He was a first-class workman, honest, strong and able at his job, so good that he had to be put in the middle of the gang because he went too fast for the rest. He was a happy man as long as he lived. Today he would have been in an institution.

Dr. William Edwards, a retired general practitioner emphasized this point in the press recently. Too many people who are eccentric, and some who are considered "loonie" are put away in mental hospitals. "If your wife barks like a dog," he says, "buy her some dog biscuits. And if your son thinks he's Julius Caesar, ask him for a signed copy of his Gallic Wars."

He quotes the case of a girl named Joan. "She had a thing about undies," he writes. "She would take them off and, garbed only in her dress, present them to any likely stranger."

Her mother could have stopped her buying any more undies or she could have joined Women's Lib. But her father thought it all a scandal and now she languishes in some institution. Doctors do try to keep these people at home, but their families just won't love them, understand them or accept them.

Why can't our society treat these very nice people as the village used to treat its idiot? Must they moulder in great barracks, having group therapy, aversion therapy, electric shocks? Does it do anybody any good?

BIZARRE ENTERTAINMENTS

The Pigtail Organ
A Taste for Fire and Bicycles
The Ferret-Packers
Crazy Contests
The Welly, the Haggis and the Flitch
All the Fun of the Fake
Strong Stuff
An Unusual Museum
Anything for Novelty
Tattoo!
Hail Dracula! Hail Frankenstein!
Embarrassment or Bonanza?
Audience Participation
Postscript

BIZARRE ENTERTAINMENTS

The Pigtail Organ

The year was 1851 and the Great Exhibition in Hyde Park, London, had drawn people from the ends of the earth to see the wonders of art and science destined, so the Prince Consort hoped and believed, to usher in an era of world peace and plenty.

Mr. Thomas Cook ran special excursions from the provinces so that villagers from afar could gape at the wonders of civilization. Flags flew and crowds on foot, in coaches and in private carriages flocked all the way along Piccadilly, under the arches of elms in the Park to see the dreamlike Palace of Glass that housed all the marvels of the century.

They entered, sauntered along the aisles and gazed in amazement. Then, at one point, a curious sound arose and a crowd began to gather round the organ-like structure from which it appeared to emanate.

No *vox humana, gamba* or *diapason* this, only a succession of squeals which nevertheless built up into a melody that they could all recognize. This was the famous Pigtail Organ whose sounds were provided by a small herd of pigs each having a differently pitched squeal. To the tail of each one was attached a squeezer operated by a single key of the organ. The organist could sit at his console and, when he pressed the keys in succession, the pigs would do the rest, producing melody, sometimes even simple harmony, to the intense delight of the crowd.

This tail-squeezing, which would arouse a storm of objections if it were to be carried on today, does not appear to have struck the people of 1851 as being in the slightest degree cruel, at least not cruel enough to warrant prosecution under the Act of 1849.

Anything can be entertainment. The Greeks and Romans had their elaborate theatres and amphitheatres, the people of the Middle Ages their nativity and mystery plays, but the bulk of the entertainment of the common people was to be found in the streets, in the comedy and tragedy of everyday life. Take a scene in medieval London, recorded in the Chronicles of the Grey Friars:

> "This yeere was a Cooke boyld in a Caldron in Smythfielde for he would a-poysoned the Bishop of Rochester, with dyvers of his Servants; and he was lockd in a Chain, and pulld up and down with a Gibbet, at dyvers Tymes, til he was dede."

Or read of the penance imposed on the Duchess of Gloucester, wife of Duke Humphrey, who in 1441 had tried to cause the death of King Henry VI by witchcraft. On three separate days she was made to walk barefoot through the London streets clad in a white sheet and carrying a wax taper weighing two pounds while all the streets were crowded and curious eyes stared out from every window.

A Taste for Fire and Bicycles

The theatre even today is only a small fraction of the entertainment world, and few of the most bizarre characters and entertainments have been seen in it. Some, more curious than ever do appear on the stage or are to be seen among the buskers who perform outside the gallery doors to keep the queues happy until opening time.

Thus it has always been. One of the most famous figures of the 17th century was Richardson the Fire-Eater whose performance even today would be considered sensational. He chewed and swallowed hot coals and ate molten glass, then continued his meal by putting a hot coal on his tongue and on top of that an oyster. Coal and oyster were then blown by bellows until the oyster was cooked and Richardson proceeded to swallow oyster, coal and all. The meal was finished off with a draught of a flaming mixture of pitch, wax and sulphur. A fake? Who knows? Had he been living in the 20th century he would certainly have made a name for himself.

Other people have done so. At the eleventh Festival of Silly Records in France in March, 1977, the stuntman Michel Lotito, better known to his friends as Monsieur Mange-tout (Eat-all), set a record by eating eight pounds of bicycle including tyre material and pump within a fortnight. He said the easiest part to eat was the chain because it tasted better than the rest and the coating of grease helped it to slide down more easily.

In 1978, he beat his own record at a fair by eating more than 15 pounds of bicycle cut into chunks, in 12 days, and was paid £2,500 ($5,000) for the feat. As side dishes he got down 100 razor blades, two plates and a glass.

"When I was young," he told reporters, "I had a complex—I was too thin. When I was sixteen I ate my first piece of glass in a swimming pool. Then I ate plates, nails, bottles, all to win bets."

Later he hoped to eat a television set, the third he will have tackled, and after that he wants to eat a small plane.

Compared with these two men the Roman glutton Arpocras, who is said to have at one sitting devoured four tablecloths and a broken glass, was a mere tyro.

Today, public eating contests are fairly common, but none can beat for ingenuity the trick played some 200 years ago by a London worker who offered to wager that he and a friend would eat a bushel of tripe and drink four bottles of wine within an hour. He was taken on by a large number of onlookers, then sat down at table while the dish and four bottles were brought in. He took a plate of the tripe and emptied half a bottle of wine into his glass, demolished these, then poured all the rest of the wine into the dish of tripe and brought in his friend—a brown bear. The tripe and wine rapidly vanished leaving the trickster many pounds better off.

The Ferret-Packers

In England during the last decade there has been a craze as to who can keep ferrets down his trousers for the longest period of time. The ferret, as is well known, is a little animal used by gamekeepers and others for driving out the rabbits from their warrens to be killed. The ferret has needle-sharp teeth, a most unpleasant disposition and is apt to get nasty when cornered. And what more disagreeable corner for an ill-tempered ferret than down a man's trousers?

One of the earliest exponents of the game was Silvester McCoy, part of whose "turn" was to put one of these animals down his trousers and keep it there for half a minute. In 1971 Paul Wells of Camborne in Cornwall got his mates to tie up his trouser legs at the bottom, then slipped his pet ferret, Whitey, in at the top, keeping him there for all of one minute.

"The other blokes were scared to touch the ferret," he said. "It felt awful. It wriggled backwards and forwards as far as it could go. Then it scratched my leg. I was waiting every second for that bite. I hoped and prayed it would never happen. You can't trust a ferret, no matter how quiet it is."

Then in 1977 Phil Smith and his mate Tony Tuthill attempted to break the record and managed the staggering total of 4½ hours!

So we go on. Any challengers?

Crazy Contests

There is in Europe a high-rating television programme called IT'S A KNOCKOUT in which all the stars, if they can be so called, are ordinary people from the various nations who have never been seen on the screen before, and who play the most extraordinary team games—the more absurd the better. The enthusiastic reception of this programme and its retention as a TV feature is an acknowledgment of the entertainment value of popular competitions in the unusual.

The same is happening in the U.S. At the beginning of 1978 the *San Francisco Sun* published its list of Crazy Contests of that year. Among those in February came the International Pancake Race between Liberal, Kansas, and Olney, England, where it has been carried on for the last 500 years or more. Women contestants in both places have to dash 415 yards on an S-shaped course all the while flipping a pancake in a frying-pan. A transatlantic phone call giving times decides on the world champion's name. This in Kansas has only been going on for 30 years but, as the newspaper says, experience doesn't seem to matter much.

In the same month came the elephant, ostrich and camel races at Indio, California, "and there's no telling when a camel will take over and do what it pleases."

In March came the Gold-Panning Contests at Rosamund, California; in April the World Heavyweight Ski Contests in Carrabassett Valley, Maine, in which every entrant has to weigh at least 225 lbs. (16 stones 1 lb.).

In May at Beaver, Oklahoma, came the World's Cowchip-Throwing Contest. "Our pioneer ancestors discovered that there was a lot of fun to be had in loading wagons with the stuff—all you had to do was to make a game out of it. And that's just what goes on in Beaver where they call cowchips Nature's Frisbees. For a $5 entry you get two cowchips, minimum 6 inches in diameter and the right to see how far you can fling 'em. The world's record stands at 193 feet."

They have advanced a good deal in this particular sport since 1971 when Governor David Hall of Oklahoma recorded a distance of 94 feet with a hand-sized cowpat and was in 1972 soundly trounced by former Governor Dewey Bartlett who shattered all records with a breathtaking 138 feet. His great achievement was watched by a crowd of 1500.

June sees the International Chicken Flying Meet at Rio Grande, Ohio, and the Watermelon Seed-Spitting Contests at Monticello, Florida. In July and August these are held at Lulling, Texas, and at Southwestern Oklahoma State University.

In July contestants brave the Colorado River on a 7-mile stretch in auto-truck inner tubes; there is the Tom Sawyer Fence-Painting Contest at Hannibal, Missouri; and at Mackinac Island, Michigan, they skip stones over the surface of the water. "For a quarter you get six stones to skip. The recognized world record is 19 pitty-pats. You may as well start learning the lingo. A pitty-pat is a short skip, a plink is a broad skip, a plonk is a shot that skips into a wave, and a skronker is an effort that misses the water completely and hits a spectator."

August sees a Fishworm Judging Contest at Sterling, Colorado; and at Pasadena, California, are the world Frisbee Championships; September the Turkey Races at Montgomery, Indiana; October a Wrist-Wrestling Tournament at Petaluma, California; and a National Oyster-Shucking Championship at Leonardstown, Maryland.

Traditional entertainments are not all dead. Where they are dead, new ones are invented, and such is the popular enthusiasm for them that they soon become traditional in their own right.

The Welly, the Haggis and the Flitch

The British can go a long way towards rivalling these zany public contests. In ancient Greece athletes used to throw the discus; today the place of the discus has been usurped in popular sport at least by the humble "welly."

What the Iron Duke would say if he could see the aristocratic boot named after him grabbed by the leg-piece and merrily flung around, we can't say, but the wellington, a boot once sported by the best society, is today worn by the ploughman, the cleaner of drains and anybody who has to trudge through deep mud. Welly-flinging may never supplant the discus in the Olympics, but it's fun.

Haggis is a traditional Scottish dish made from the heart, liver, lungs and sometimes the small intestines of the calf or sheep, boiled in the animal's stomach with a seasoning of pepper, salt, onions, etc., chopped fine with oatmeal. It was first made by poor crofters' and farmers' wives and is now a national dish used at functions and celebrations as well as in the home.

There is in Sutherland a derelict village named Auchnaclory whose menfolk used to earn a living from the adjacent hill pastures. At midday when they came down to the village for a meal their wives would bring the haggis for their lunch as far as the stream then, standing on a rock, fling it across to them.

From these small beginnings the sport of throwing the haggis has spread to many parts of Scotland. It was taken up by a public relations officer who made up an elaborate set of rules for the game. It is played as follows:

Before the hurl the Haggis Hooter is sounded. The women then bring the $1\frac{1}{2}$-lb. haggis to the hurlers and they have to stand on the Hurling Barrel which represents the rock on which the women stood in olden times. One rule is that the haggis must be intact on landing—a commonsense one for the original throwers if the lunch was not to be scattered among the heather and lost.

Once the rules had been made, the contests caught on like wildfire. Teams began to play home and away matches as in football and rugby. They soon attracted thousands of followers and an association was formed. New methods of throwing the haggis were evolved; the sport was first tried out officially in 1977 at the International Gathering of the Clans and a world record of about 150 feet has been set up.

Even if it was desirable there is no way of stopping this game though the sponsorship originally given by J & B Whisky has now been withdrawn. The public relations officer who made up the rules says, "When I make my first million I'll have a golden haggis on the mantelpiece."

The oldest contest of all and bizarre enough in its way is the one between sets of married couples for the Dunmow Flitch. To win the Flitch of Bacon a couple have to prove that "they have lived together a twelvemonth and a day without any quarrel or any wish to be unmarried."

The contest goes back almost a thousand years to the time when the Church was concerned at the casual way among the Saxon people that married couples lived as man and wife. To show divine approval for partners in a good and lasting marriage they awarded a prize—a flitch or flank of bacon. As one old Essex labourer put it:

"Them ancient folks—maybe the Romans—guv a bit o'bacon to them as didn't whop their missus."

The contests were first carried on by the priors of Little Dunmow in Essex and soon became major entertainments, attracting people from all over the countryside around as well as showmen and mountebanks who found this a fine pretext for holding small fairs for buying and selling, and for starting all kinds of sideshows.

The cases were tried by a judge and a jury of six bachelors and six maidens; witnesses were brought forward and there were two counsels, one for the claimants, the other for the "bacon." These cross-examined claimants and witnesses and addressed the jury. An old injunction to the claimants runs:

"You shall swear by the Custom of our Confession
That you never made any nuptial Transgression
Since you were married Man and Wife
By household Brawls or contentious Strife
Or otherwise in Bed or at Board
Offended each other in Deed or Word."

When the names of the winners were proclaimed they were carried in a chair borne by eight men to the festivities.

There was great fun at these trials but detailed cross-examination was an ordeal and most couples took it seriously. In days when prices were rising, a free flitch of bacon was worth a fight. But if by chance the Counsel for the Bacon revealed the slightest deviation from the straight and narrow path all prospects of winning could vanish. One man, an ambulance driver, had to admit that he had women as workmates—black mark number one; also that at the station there was only one common lavatory—black mark number two. Both he and his wife had to proclaim complete trust and devotion in spite of this evidence.

Early flitch contests were held in many parts of England and even as far away as Vienna. In 1905 a ceremony of the same kind took place in New York when the flitch was won by Walter Girdwood Mulliner and Gabrielle, his wife, "in reverence for the old tradition, its quaint basic thought so sweetly resting in the sanctity of the marriage relation, knowing in their hearts that they earned the Flitch of Bacon . . ."

All the Fun of the Fake

"There are wonders and beasts exhibited, a camel, a girl without bones, the dancing mare; the child born back to back with a live bear, the double girl, the man with one head and two bodies, the man whose body was only 21 inches high but his arms of ordinary length; the grimacing Spaniard; the fairy 150 years of age; the German woman with no hands or feet; the transparent child; the child with three legs."

"Here's Whittington's cat and the tall dromedary,
The chaise without horses, and Queen of Hungary;
The famed learnèd dog that can tell all his letters;
And some men, as scholars, are not much his betters."

This was Bartholomew Fair, held every August until 1859 outside St. Bartholomew the Great in Smithfield, London. Here a whole minor industry was devoted to satisfying the popular demand to see freaks, oddities and wonders.

Hardly a country fair in the old days but had its freak show, its fat ladies and six-legged sheep. One little boy, wonderstruck at what he had seen in one of these shows, couldn't believe it was all genuine and determined to find out for himself. So, after standing around for a long time in front of the booth he managed to make friends with the barker and one day, after the handbell had stopped ringing and the crowd had gone in they began to talk. The boy saw his chance. Were the strange creatures real? If they were, why was nobody allowed to touch them?

The barker thought a minute, then replied,

"Touch them? You couldn't do that."

"But are they real then?" persisted the boy.

The barker looked round cautiously, then bent down and almost whispered in the boy's ear, "Don't say ought, lad, but y'can do a lot wi' papermash. Now get along."

The barker would say no more and the boy went away disconsolate. Papermash! It was years before he realized what the barker had been talking about.

Strong Stuff

The craze for the unusual remains as keen as ever. Some years ago the late Mr. Robert L. Ripley, collector of oddities, ran cartoons in several weekly newspapers under the title *Believe It or Not.* In 1971 Mr. T. Alec Rigby, director of the Canadian company, Ripley International, had no fewer than seven exhibitions of Mr. Ripley's wonders which he called Odditoriums, in America and Canada, and began the setting up of the eighth on Blackpool's Golden Mile. He spent £250,000 renovating a public house for the staging of it and planned to stock it with half a million pounds' worth of bizarre exhibits.

"It's not what you put on show," he said, "it's how you do it. It's the way we display each item and create the right atmosphere. For instance, in the catacombs where the theme is torture we play very strange stereo music and bongo drums."

Among other items are a thimble full of 10,000 tiny nuts and bolts, oil paintings on pinheads, the world's strangest graveyard with peculiar epitaphs, a grandfather clock made entirely out of seashells, a shrunken head and a wax model of the famous double-eyed Lee Ching, Governor of Shansi Province in Imperial China who had two pupils in each eye.

Much more eerie in the same Golden Mile was the Temple of Black Magic run by Lord Thomas Howard—his real name this, not a title—with Zola the Zombie, Lola the pocket-sized Venus in a goldfish bowl, the Bride of Frankenstein, Dante's Inferno and the Half Man, Half Woman.

An inquisitive visitor asked him where he got his exhibits.

"Oh, I think them up," replied Lord Thomas.

Strong stuff this. The great American showman Phineas T. Barnum knew how to produce it. In 1898 his show included a man who looked like a Skye terrier; a woman with a goatee; a blue man (who had previously dyed himself by accident with silver nitrate); the most tattooed woman in the world who claimed to have been stabbed by the needle 100 million times; a Ubangi with saucers in both top and bottom lips; an "India-rubber man" who could pull the skin several inches off his cheeks; a woman whom nobody could make laugh (because her facial muscles were paralyzed); a "hard-headed man" on whose 2-inch-thick skull people could break blocks of granite; an ossified man whose flesh had completely hardened and crystallized before he died; a living skeleton weighing 70 pounds that stood 6 feet tall; a "gorilla girl" billed as the ugliest woman in the world; and "What-is-it?" a congenital idiot so misshapen and retarded that people believed him to be an unknown species of monkey.

Nobody has ever found a mermaid but Barnum created one. Experts said that it was made from a bit of orang-outang stuck on to the lower half of some salmon-like fish or other.

"Never underestimate the intelligence of the public," Barnum is reported to have said.

He didn't. When the mermaid was shown in London three or four hundred people a day paid a shilling each to see it.

One of the books Barnum wrote was entitled *The Humbugs of the World.* He didn't mind being one himself; it made him very rich.

An Unusual Museum

One of the least entertaining aspects of human life is the paying of taxes. It is something we all have to do so we may as well see the humorous side of it. Rotterdam in Holland has its own special kind of Odditorium devoted to taxes and nothing else.

It was founded in 1936 by Dr. J. van der Poel, himself a tax collector who saw its educational as well as its humorous value, for he had exhibits of every possible phase of taxation going right back to the beginnings of recorded time. For instance, you can see a hieroglyphic-inscribed Egyptian stone from 2,100 B.C. that was hung by a thong from a sheep's neck to indicate proof of tax payment on sheep. There is an etching by Rembrandt showing Christ holding a coin used for tribute money. Perhaps the most appropriate painting is an oil by the Italian Pietro Mattani which shows a revenue officer presenting a tax bill to a poor tailor while the tailor's wife, hands defiantly on her hips, is looking daggers at the collector.

The museum has the largest collection of tax stamps, the earliest one invented by a Dutchman in 1624, and there is another section lodged in the basement given over to clever frauds, especially the devices used by smugglers to avoid paying customs duties—a teddy bear which had a belly full of Swiss watches, a walking cane and a rubber tyre that had been hollowed out so as to smuggle gin, false noses, scooped-out books, shoes with secret compartments, balls of knitting wool that had been filled with narcotics and Christmas ornaments used to smuggle liquor.

The comic section is worth the price of admission—about 5p (10 cents) tax free, for there are more than 5,000 cartoons from all around the world that have been collected from as far back as the 19th century. Three of the funniest, all from the United States have captions. In the first a husband says to his wife that the Revenue want to know where he gets his money to pay his taxes; the second features a drinker who accuses the Revenue Department of putting a tax on drink, then raises all the other taxes to help drive people to it; and the third shows a man blowing his nose and claiming the Internal Revenue is printing its new tax forms on Kleenex to keep taxpayers comfortable while they pay through the nose.

"There are two words beginning with the syllable *tax*," says Mark Twain, "*taxpayer* and *taxidermist*. The difference between them is that the latter takes only your skin."

Anything for Novelty

American television producers have recently had to face the fact that well-known stars, shy of over-exposure to the cameras which may affect their popularity ratings adversely, are turning down invitations to appear on talk shows. To keep them going the producers are having to turn to another kind of entertainer—the zany, and the daffier he is the better. Anybody who had an unusual act of any kind was invited by advertisements in local papers to offer it.

Applications were legion. There was the mid-western lawyer who could press the palms of his hands together then squeeze out the air so that he could play the "Stars and Stripes Forever"; "Gypsy Rose Knee" who told fortunes by examining the knees of her clients; a man from Texas whose cow could foretell the weather; the Eskimo Olympic team that held an ear-pulling contest; and a man who rented out space on his bald head for advertising, then walked around almost doubled over near the supermarkets. There were extra-fat ladies who sang and did precision dancing at the same time—unusual among people with weight problems; and the joker who could blow up hot water bottles till they burst.

Animal acts were plentiful. There were singing frogs which, it was said, performed better on the phone than on the air; the chicken that played *tic tac toe;* the frisbee-catching dog and the man-wrestling kangaroo. Appearing on British TV are melodious dogs who perform to strains on the piano; and recently viewers have been treated to both a duck and a dog performing on the skateboard.

One of the most notable of these bizarre entertainers is Stephen Weisberg who told the interviewer that he did impressions of motor cars—not of the noise they make but of what they look like. He has a repertoire of twenty domestic and foreign cars of the '40s and '50s that he can "do" just by pulling faces. "I can do tail-lights too," he boasts.

When as a boy he went out with his parents, he noticed that every car had its own characteristic expression just as animals have. For instance, he said, a '52 Buick looked like Lon Chaney in "Phantom of the Opera." Then when he was 24 a number of illustrated car books came into his hands and that was the real beginning of his act.

This is more than just fun to Stephen Weisberg. "I am a serious entertainer," he says. "I am making a statement about the love affair the American people have for their cars."

A more off-putting guest was Brother Theodore whose speciality was giving people frights. In an interview he would act for a few minutes in a perfectly normal and restrained manner, then, with no warning at all he would go into a terrific rage, stamping, ranting and shrieking in German at the top of his voice.

"We just didn't know what to do," said his interviewer. "We didn't even know if what he said was fit to be broadcast. Anyway he told us that he'd scared away muggers with his act, and that's something."

Then there was Omar the beggar who taught people how to feign blindness and pretend to be crippled so that they could be successful as beggars. There's nothing new in that however, Elizabethan England had thousands of *abram-men* and *dummerers*—beggars who pretended to be mad or dumb—*whipjacks* who feigned wounds inflicted in the wars, *fraters* or mock priests, rogues, ruffians, and bawdy-baskets. The highways were alive with them.

Some of the turns interviewed for the talk shows were quite unacceptable. One who nearly made it, but not quite, was the man who claimed to be the world's biggest eater, so they brought him $700 (£300) worth of food from a top Los Angeles restaurant, fully expecting a TV star to emerge.

He started eating, went on eating—and eating—and eating. But this was for a talk show, and when he was eating he couldn't talk. Their $700 were wasted.

Down curtains!

Tattoo!

On Friday the 31st of March 1978, San Francisco added one more to its long list of bizarre events. This was the first Annual Tattoo Ball when some 350 tattooers and "tattooees" plus an equal number of spectators attended; admission $7 with $1 refund to those who could display a tattoo. The ball was organized by tattooist Lyle Tuttle and attended by notables from all walks of life, described in the *San Francisco Chronicle* as "bikers, businessmen and gay blades, housewives, hookers and molls of every description vying for attention from the ubiquitous TV cameras . . ."

The veteran of the show was Miss Bobby Librarry, described as the Fairy Godmother of the Tattoo Art Museum who at 84 was said to be perhaps the most venerable tattooed lady in the world. Though old, blind in one eye and deaf in one ear she was nevertheless perched on a chair while admirers, photographers and a man with a magnifying glass perused the now-flaccid but once-brilliant designs on her skin.

Let the *Chronicle* tell the rest of the story:

"The lady who calls herself Satana Starslick parades the lobby . . . with statuesque composure, flashbulbs illuminating her pathway.

"She is wearing a black, off-one-shoulder leotard top which sags under the weight of her abundant bosom and a black mini-skirt slit to her waist. Much of the skin visible on her bared shoulder, arms, thigh and leg is tattooed with dragons, flowers, and abstract expressionist meanderings in blues, blacks and reds. She moves with regal authority like the tattoo queen she is.

"Satana Starslick pauses periodically in her travels to dole dollops of discourse to a dozen diligent reporters. 'I am a tattoo artist,' she announces. 'I'm 22. I got my first tattoo when I was nine . . .'

"The entertainers included Nicholas Gravenites, Mark Naftalin, Anna Rizzo, Pee Wee Ellis, Rene LeBallister, Snooky Flowers and Smoke George and the Superstars, belly dancer Khadija and Martha the opera singer who was wearing a push-up bra the better to lend proper curvature to the tattooed flower peeking out from deep within her cleavage . . .

"I wandered over to Khadija, who offers, according to her card, 'High Energy Belly Dance Instruction.' Khadija is probably the most tattooed belly dancer this side of Istanbul. 'It's a hobby with me,' she said brightly, exhibiting shoulders beladen with Japanese flora. 'I won *Best on a Woman* at the 1977 Tattoo Convention in Reno. It gives my mother nightmares . . .'"

Not only your mother, I'm afraid.

Hail Dracula! Hail Frankenstein!

In 1897 Bram Stoker published his horror story *Dracula*. For more than a generation the tale of the legendary Count of Terror lay almost unread on library shelves. Then, after World War I when stories of ghouls and ghosties became the vogue, the Transylvanian nobleman emerged from the shades. Stoker had produced a belated best-seller.

It is now more than 80 years since he chose the North Yorkshire town of Whitby as the setting for the vampire count's arrival in England from his Transylvanian homeland, and it was fitting that his fans, members of the Dracula Society, should hold in 1977 a Vampires' Celebration Ball to commemorate the 80th anniversary of that momentous first night when Dracula was entertained, at the Royal Hotel in that town.

It was a great event. Besides Dracula himself, Frankenstein's monster also graced the gathering with his presence, together with a multitude of ghouls, a walking corpse and a number of assorted vampires who had hopped, crawled and flapped their way from all parts of Britain to pay respects to their idol. All night long they danced the Stomp, the Monster Mash, and a variety of spine-chilling capers.

Everybody, if you'll pardon the expression, had a bloody good time and, shortly before sunrise a vote of fangs (pardon again!) was proposed to their gruesome and ungenial host.

Monsters are the rage. They pitchfork us out of the boredom of everyday life into an imaginary world where our subconscious fears can be overcome. The hair stands on end, the flesh creeps, teeth chatter and the blood runs cold. And we revel in it. It is good therapy because we know that we can always come back, just when we feel like it, to our dear familiar, humdrum, everyday life.

That's probably why Keith Reber and his girl-friend (or should we say ghoul-friend) Katherine Engel celebrated the world's most horrible marriage ceremony, joining themselves in unholy matrimony in Los Angeles.

They were specially made up for the event by experts at the Universal Studios as Frankenstein's Monster and his Bride. Superior Court Commissioner Robert B. Axel dutifully married them in a short service, a "werewolf" acting as chief witness. They sealed the nuptials with a waxy kiss, cut a ghoulish cake and toasted each other with blood-red cocktails. Then the Monster with his awful wedded wife drove off for their honeymoon in a hearse.

Their grandchildren are sure to enjoy looking at the wedding photographs.

Embarrassment or Bonanza?

In show business, things are sure to go wrong occasionally, as they did at one of Lancashire's Agricultural Fairs.

As a relief from the serious job of contemplating the good and bad points of cattle, sheep and pigs, a number of sideshows are usually set up at such fairs by various outside organizations.

One of these was the Cheshire Baptists' Association who decided to put on a tableau of the Ideal Bible Family. The scene was to be a room in a humble home with members of the family round the table—first the father, a sturdy and stern head of the family, beside him his homely, submissive wife; and between the two their sweet innocent daughter. All three gazed intently on a page of the opened family Bible, while at the side, pointing with his finger at the chosen passage was a pious and dignified Baptist minister.

The problem for the Baptist Association was to get suitable figures for the tableau. Luckily there was, not far away in Blackpool, a Madame Tussaud's Wax Museum, whose manager they approached and found more than willing to support such a good cause. Eventually the dummies, fully dressed, arrived, the scene was set up and the characters arranged in their places at the table exactly according to plan.

The sideshow was an instant draw, but for the wrong reasons. It soon dawned on the first visitors to see it that the figure of the minister in the tableau was none other than that of the notorious murderer Dr. Crippen; the father a well-known swindler; the mother a composite of the Queen's body and the head of a famous woman ice-skater; while the daughter had the figure and face of Snow White.

There may have been a few red faces, but the Baptist Tableau was a complete success.

Audience Participation

The success of any show or competition depends on how far the audience can be persuaded to "go with" the performer. Even though they may hardly move or make a sound a performer knows from the start whether they are with him or not, and how much response he is likely to get from them.

Response comes in many forms—the quiet titter, the burst of laughter, stamping of the feet, clapping, whistling, joining in the chorus or even taking an active part in the show itself as often happens with TV audiences.

And, as everybody knows, it can be managed.

In the early years of the 19th century an office was opened in Paris which could, on application, supply any amount of professional applause for singers, actors or managers who were willing to pay for it.

This consisted of fixed numbers of hirelings who would start the applause and lead it at various prearranged points in the show, or at other places where there was promise of audience reaction. These professional applauders were called *claqueurs* (*claquer*—to clap).

In the case of humorous turns or sketches, laughter was needed more than formal applause, and so it was possible to hire *rieurs* (*rire*—to laugh) who could be relied on to do their job lightly, moderately or uproariously at just the right places.

In the case of tragedy, *pleureurs* (*pleurer*—to weep) were needed who could accompany tears with the required wailing—not too little, not too much.

Or, if a song, dance or act required an encore, a few *biseurs* were hired to shout "Bis! Bis!" or "Encore! Encore!"

If you had the money you could pay for a good start to a season, and often a good start guaranteed a good long run. A group of these professional applauders was and is still called a *claque* and is hired to be present in some countries at many a public show and not a few political conventions.

They are the daddies and mammies of all cheerleaders.

Postscript

Those who have visited Oberammergau at the time of the Passion Play see something of the drama of the Passion as portrayed by the people of this Bavarian village. Unfortunately it is the cause of a few minor dramas of passion among the inhabitants themselves.

The 1,600 or so villagers are not due to present their next Play until 1980, but already some romantic young males are complaining that love affairs are almost impossible. This is because so many young maidens aspire to play the part of the Virgin Mary.

It has been so since the original performance in 1684. The present barriers will not be down until the part has been cast. Even here the course of true love does not always run smoothly!

BIZARRE FRAUD

The Sheer Nerve of the Con Man

The Man Who Sold Nelson's Column
Fraud in a Baker's Shop
"I Have Paid—but!"
Fancy Titles at a Fancy Price
Fraud by Numbers
Confidence "Par Excellence"
Imposters
The Bogus Doctor
The Home-Grabbers
Tragic Young Genius
Shakespeare Rediscovered
The Counterfeiters
An Ill-Defined Boundary
To What End?

BIZARRE FRAUD

THE SHEER NERVE OF THE CON MAN

Crime is always a serious business but it can have its amusing side (though this may not always be appreciated by the victim). Part of its amusing nature arises from the ingenious ruses invented at times by those who commit it. On this account one does not often find the bizarre among the straightforward crimes, such as street violence and even manslaughter, which by their very nature are not planned beforehand in any great detail. Kidnapping, conspiracy, forgery, theft and murder give more examples of the bizarre, mainly because of the thought that often has to be put into them before the commission. But the richest harvest of all is to be found among the stories of confidence trickery and fraud. Some of them leave us amazed that anybody could have the cheek, self-possession and effrontery to conceive and execute such apparently mad schemes.

The Man Who Sold Nelson's Column

One of the world's most expert confidence tricksters was Arthur Furguson and he, if we are to believe the accounts, got into the business purely by accident. One day in London, seeing an American visitor looking up at the statue of Nelson on top of the column in Trafalgar Square, he suddenly had the idea of selling it.

He found it easy enough to strike up an acquaintance with his prospective victim and was soon explaining how this column was the nation's memorial to Horatio Nelson, one of the greatest of all English admirals who lost his life in command of the fleet at the battle of Trafalgar, etcetera, etcetera, etcetera. But alas, it was now having to be sold. As all Americans knew, the British between 1914 and 1918 had fought a costly war which had left the country deeply in debt. How was the Government to get out of the mess? It was sad, but Nelson, like many more of the national treasures, would just have to go.

The American visitor was full of sympathy for the plight of the British, but that didn't blind him to the chance of a profitable business deal. Did Mr. Furguson know the price?

Yes, indeed, replied Furguson, providing the right buyer could be found—somebody who would treat the memory of this great British hero with due respect and see that the statue was well preserved and cared for. In fact, he had himself been entrusted by the Government to find the right buyer. Of course, there were many interested parties, and once the secret got out there would be no difficulty at all in selling. But so far nothing was settled; in fact the whole business was being kept quiet until the last minute—national pride, you know.

The price? A mere £6,000 ($30,000) which might possibly include Landseer's four lions at the base for the buyer who could provide the necessary guarantees.

The American was eager. Could Furguson help him to clinch the deal immediately?

Well, such a thing was rarely done; it wasn't the British way but, if he could be given a few minutes to phone his superiors at the Board of Works and Public Buildings there might be a remote chance. The deal would naturally require the consent of the Treasury, but that could possibly be arranged at the same time.

The American fell in with the idea and Furguson went off to find a telephone booth. In a few minutes he returned. He had spoken to his bosses and obtained verbal permission. All that was needed was to pass over the cheque for the £6,000. Of course, there would be the job of removing the column, but the Government could help; it had a number of contractors on its books.

The gullible tourist handed over a cheque and the two parted. Then he rang the contractors whose name Furguson had given him. They knew nothing about it, couldn't believe that he had bought the column and advised him to get in touch with Scotland Yard. He soon realized that he had been fooled and there was little hope of tracing the man who had fooled him. By this time Furguson had already got away.

In a very short time he was on the lookout for more dupes. Later in the same summer he received a deposit of £1,000 on the sale of Big Ben and another of £2,000 for Buckingham Palace. He was never arrested in England.

In 1925 he was in the United States, leased to a dupe the White House for $100,000 a year and persuaded an Australian to raise another $100,000 pending the drawing up of a contract for the removal of the Statue of Liberty in order to widen New York Harbor. The Australian had difficulty in raising the money, and Furguson pressed him for it so that he became suspicious and informed the police. Luckily for him he could show them a photograph that had been taken of him with Furguson in front of the Statue of Liberty.

That was the end—for a time. Furguson was arrested and served five years, but he had learned enough to know that a persuasive tongue pays dividends. He lived to bring off more swindles and to retire to Los Angeles where he died in 1938.

The same kind of ruse was carried off by Count Victor Lustig, who pretended to be a high official of the French Government but who, with the help of Dan Collins, a small-time American crook who posed as his secretary, sold the Eiffel Tower *twice*, the first time to a Paris businessman for high-grade scrap. Fearing the ridicule of the business world the buyer never reported the hoax. The second time the tower was sold the hoax was reported but the two hoaxers got away. After that the police were more vigilant and the same kind of trick has not been tried since.

Fraud in a Baker's Shop

One of the most amusing of all petty crimes was committed in London more than 650 years ago.

In those days people had fires in their houses but few had ovens, so it was customary for them to knead their dough at home, then to take it to the baker's shop to be made into loaves and baked.

They usually brought it in bowls which the baker emptied on to his table or "molding-board" on which he shaped the dough into loaves, then passed them on to his journeyman or to an apprentice who looked after the oven.

In 1327 one of these bakers, John Brid, got the brilliantly crooked idea of cutting a small circular hole in the molding-board, which could be stopped with a plug and which, in the half-dark of the shop, would not be noticed by his customers. Under the table was one of his assistants who, as soon as the dough flopped on to the table, took out the plug,

> "which servant of his, so seated beneath the hole and carefully opening it, piecemeal and bit by bit craftily withdrew some of the dough aforesaid, frequently collecting great quantities from such dough falsely, wickedly and maliciously; to the great loss of all his neighbours and persons living near." (Riley, *Memorials of London*)

In time, some of the customers, wondering why they were getting less bread in quantity than they should, went to the Guildhall and the Mayor then sent his serjeant, his clerk and one of his sheriffs to the shop while the business was in full swing. The baker and his assistants were caught red-handed, the table pushed aside and the young man with the dough found underneath it.

I Have Paid—but!

Few people today remember the name of Horatio William Bottomley, but in the early years of the century his name in Britain was a household word. Born in 1860, he was for a time in business in London, then took to journalism and founded the *Financial Times.*

He was best known for the weekly journal *John Bull* which was nothing short of his own personal mouthpiece, spreading abroad the views of Horatio Bottomley and little else. On its cover appeared the well-known title-figure—a stout English gentleman in tall hat, frock-coat and high boots carrying a switch, with his bulldog by his side. With it was the four-line piece of doggerel—

"The world is a bundle of hay;
Mankind are the asses who pull.
Each pulls it a different way,
But the greatest of all is John Bull."

Bottomley feared nobody. His attacks on politicians and public bodies who fell short in his opinion in any way, were bitter and often verged on libel, sometimes landing him in court. But he was an expert at getting out of trouble, a plausible speaker who became famous for conducting his own defence. From 1906 until 1912 and again from 1918 to 1922 he was M.P. for South Hackney, London, a position Bottomley used to further his over-riding interest—his own fortune, fame, influence and popularity.

One of his many sidelines was the turf and, as owner of a string of racehorses he got the idea, shortly before the First World War, of arranging things in such a way that every horse would arrive at the winning-post in the order he wanted, thus giving him the certainty of winning a fortune.

Such a scheme would have been impossible to carry out in Britain where the rules were very strict, so he decided on Blankenberghe in Belgium, choosing a single race in which none but his own horses would be entered and in which the jockeys he employed would have instructions to bring them in in a certain order. In this way Bottomley and all those who were in the know and had helped him could lay heavy bets and sweep the board.

It didn't happen that way. Midway through the race a sea-mist came in, blocking the view along part of the course so that the jockeys lost sight of one another, getting hopelessly out of order. They finished quite differently from what had been expected. Bottomley and his cronies, instead of picking up fortunes, lost heavily.

Fancy Titles at a Fancy Price

In Germany you could become a member of a learned society, a doctor, a professor or even a knight, provided you had the money. The man who could get it for you was Hans Weyer.

In the 1960's he arranged to take 300 Germans to Syracuse Cathedral in Sicily to become knights of the Holy Order of Saint Agatha. The snag was that there was no such order in existence. That did not prevent the so-called Dr. Weyer taking from them a gross 750,000 marks—nearly £200,000 or $400,000.

Certain European countries are particularly conscious of the supposed prestige given by a title. Italians will often address Mr. Rossi, a qualified engineer, not as plain Mr. Rossi but as Ingegnere Rossi; a schoolmaster is addressed as Professore; the local police chief retains the title of Maresciallo even after he retires; and the title of Cavaliere (knight) is common; even the wife of Dottore (Dr.) So-and-so may come to be called Dottoressa by virtue of her husband's title. In Germany such titles are compounded. Doktor becomes Herr Doktor (Mr. Dr.) or Herr Professor Doktor. The General Manager of the Hamburg football team uses Doktor before his name as does the woman who reads the weather report on national television.

Titles give prestige. What a chance for the person able to sell status for money! Hans Weyer saw the possibilities and sold, on his own reckoning, 350 doctorates, 76 certificates of nobility, 80 consular titles and 23 other orders of distinction. "All my clients are sick," he said. "They require a little old-fashioned medicine. Bleeding them is my therapy." So he bled them of money and gave them in return certificates from non-existent colleges of learning such as the National College of Toronto and the Sheffield Philosophic University. Most customers asked no questions as to how the degrees, knighthoods or titles had been obtained. They knew quite well what they were doing.

Weyer was first imprisoned in Hamburg, so on his release he moved on to Munich where he could be seen driving his Rolls-Royce, handing out his private card—*Consul Hans Hermann Weyer A.D.* (*Ausser Dienst*—Retired), frequenting the best restaurants and giving liberal tips to the waiters.

One of his smartest exploits was to sell to Germany's second largest mail-order furniture dealer the title of Knight of the Orthodox Church of Cyprus. News of this made the largest dealer both angry and jealous, so he approached Weyer offering a fee of £20,000 ($40,000) to expose his rival. He was given a photograph of a waiter dressed as a priest officiating at the ceremony and he published the photo in his company's journal.

Hans Hermann Weyer is again in prison.

A degree from Yale is, of course, coveted and Yale's files of persons who have come to its attention for claiming to be alumni when they are not, number more than 7,000. Of requests that come to Stanford for substantiation of graduation an average of one in five is bogus. One man went so far as to counterfeit a University of Pennsylvania diploma claiming a degree in "negotiation administration." This, too, looked like the real thing until it was found that the President of the University had retired three years before the date of the signature that appeared on the certificate he claimed as his.

More and more public authorities and employers are becoming wise to the practice, otherwise it could end with the same state of affairs as in Gilbert and Sullivan's "wonder-working days of old," when dukes were three a penny—

"And so wherever you may be,
To this conclusion you'll agree,
When everybody's somebody
Nobody's anybody."

Fraud by Numbers

A good way of looking at a mechanical invention is to consider it as an extension of one's own physical strength which, through the muscles of the body, is controlled and directed by the human brain.

But in the last forty years ingenuity has accomplished one of the greatest feats of all time. It has extended the power of the brain itself by the invention of the computer. In other words, the computer is to the brain what the automobile, the tractor, the loom, the speedboat, the crane, the mechanical digger or the plane are to the hands and feet.

A computer will do what you tell it and ask no questions. That is, provided it has not previously been instructed to take no notice of any future programming. Experience has proved that it is impossible to foresee everything that could happen and programme a computer to prevent every possible fault. Thus, by giving instructions, an operator may enrich himself and never be found out.

This happened when a Boston bank clerk replaced blank paying-in slips on a counter with forms bearing his own account number and was credited in a very short time with hundreds of dollars. Another operator instructed a computer to take ten cents off every customer's account and credit it to the last account in the bank's alphabetical list which, of course, he held. All went well until the bank got a new customer whose name began with the letters ZY. The new customer, seeing his money growing more and more, informed the manager and the fraud was detected. It might have worked for a longer time had the operator named the last account holder Mr. Zzyzz!

Other frauds have been perpetrated in business houses by the receipt and payment of fictitious bills by computer, through creaming off discount when goods have been bought at less than the retail price, and in many other ways.

Because the operations of this ingenious extension of the human brain are so complex, these frauds are all the more difficult to detect. It is safe to say that money is at this very moment being extracted by computer fraud, by perpetrators who will never be brought to book.

Confidence "Par Excellence"

Thérèse d'Aurignac Humbert was one of the finest ladies in the Third French Republic. She was the daughter-in-law of the

Mayor of Toulouse who later became Minister of Justice, and heiress to a fortune of several millions which had been left to her by a certain Robert Henry Crawford. That at least is what everybody thought.

How this daughter of a French peasant came to maintain a luxurious establishment in Paris's Avenue de la Grande Armée, becoming one of the country's most lavish hostesses, reads like a cheap romance.

In 1879 while travelling in a surburban train she heard groans from an adjoining compartment as if some person was in distress. There was no corridor, no way of reaching that person except by opening the carriage door and scrambling along the footboard outside while the train was in motion—which she did. On entering the next compartment she found an elderly gentleman in great distress, after he had a heart attack. She administered smelling salts and gradually managed to bring him round. Thanking her profusely he took her name and address.

Two years later she received a letter from Mr. Crawford's lawyers to say that the old gentleman had died leaving her a fortune. To keep it in the family Mr. Crawford's will stated that her younger sister Marie was, when she left school, to be married to one of Mr. Crawford's two nephews. Until the wedding Thérèse was to keep the inheritance locked in a safe.

On the strength of this she borrowed colossal sums of money and moved with her husband Frédéric into the Paris mansion where they lived in great style. Then in 1883 a newspaper article appeared in which doubts were expressed as to whether the Crawford fortune really existed.

A short while after this Thérèse announced that she had broken with the Crawford brothers who had taken her to court to force her to lodge the fortune in the French bank Crédit Lyonnais. Her father-in-law's prestige as Minister of Justice had something to do with helping her to win the lawsuit.

Her difficulties were not yet over. Later she was asked by a high official of the Bank of France where the Crawford inheritance was invested. On her reply that it was in Government securities he made enquiries and found that there was no trace either of the investment or the payment of interest.

To get out of the difficulties, she then floated an insurance scheme called the Rente Viagere and this attracted large sums from investors. She used the money to pay her creditors and to buy the necessary Government securities. By this time her creditors had begun to suspect that all was not as it should be since the lawsuit and expenses connected with it must have swallowed up much of their money already. The storm broke when the newspaper *Le Matin* demanded that the safe be opened and the securities checked. She had to give way.

When the safe was opened all that was found inside was a brick and an English halfpenny.

That was in 1902. The whole story of the legacy was false. There had been no Mr. Crawford; there was not even a Crawford family and the lawsuit that had reputedly been brought by the old gentleman's nephews had been the work of her own two brothers. For *twenty years* Thérèse Humbert had lived in luxury on a fabric of lies.

By this time her husband Frédéric had died. Thérèse and her two brothers fled and for some time were nowhere to be found. They were finally tracked down and arrested in Madrid.

The Humbert scandal was the sensation of the year. During the whole of 1903 the empty safe was exhibited in a shopwindow, while Thérèse was serving the first year of a five-year sentence.

Imposters

In 1865 a young cattle-slaughterer from Wagga Wagga, Australia named Arthur Orton read an announcement inserted in a newspaper by Henrietta, Dowager Lady Tichborne, offering a reward for information about her son Roger who had been lost at sea on the ship *Bella Bella* of Liverpool eleven years earlier. Orton decided to impersonate him, made a false statement to his solicitor and raised £20,000 on the strength of his expectations. In 1866 he, his wife and baby daughter set sail for England and fortune—or so he thought.

This was the opening of the longest and most fantastic case of impersonation in English history. The hearings, which started in

1873, went on for 188 days counting the breaks, and were daily reported in the national press. They cost the Tichborne family £90,000 and ended with Orton being sentenced to 14 years in prison. As a result of the case, "false and deceitful personation of any person or of the heir, executor, administrator, wife, widow, next of kin or relative of any person" to gain money or property was made a felony punishable by penal servitude for life.

Yet, if there is one piece of advice an experienced confidence trickster could give to another, it would be this. "If you're in the fraud business it usually does pay to be somebody other than yourself." Hundreds have tried it with varying success.

In Germany before the First World War, the man most feared and respected was the army officer. Wilhelm Voigt, a shoemaker and ex-convict, planned to take advantage of this fear to rob a municipal treasury of its cash.

Dressed in a military uniform and posing as a Prussian officer, he spotted a platoon of soldiers in a Berlin street and in an angry, commanding voice called them to attention. They fell into line immediately.

A bus came along the road bound for the Köpenick district. He stood in its path, called it to a halt and bundled the men into it. When they reached their destination he lined them up again, marched them to the Mayor's office and put the mayor under arrest.

"Where is your warrant?" asked the Mayor.

"Warrant?" exclaimed the bogus captain. "*This* is my warrant!" and he waved his arm towards the platoon of soldiers.

Then he commanded the borough treasurer to hand over the whole of the cash in the safe, amounting to 4,000 marks—about $1,300 then. He marched the Mayor, Mayoress, deputy mayor and treasurer to a spot outside the Town Hall, put them under guard, ordering the men to stay at their posts for a full half-hour, and made off with the cash.

Ten days later the police arrived at Voigt's attic home and arrested him. He was jailed for four years.

The Mayor had known that he was an imposter and had told

the police. "He was rather too old for a Prussian officer," he said. "Besides, he wore his cap badge upside down."

Stephen Weinberg was a man of many parts. According to his own accounts given at various times, he had been U.S. Consul in Morocco, Peruvian Ambassador to the U.S.A., Romanian Consul-General in New York, Serbian Military Attaché in Washington, and State Department protocol expert. At one period, when he was a radio reporter in New York he saw an opportunity of becoming press officer for the Thailand Government, stating that part of his experience had been in the U.S. Office of Strategic Services during the Second World War.

In 1951 he wrote to the State Department to ask, if he took the post in the service of the Thailand Government, would he still be able to retain his American citizenship. This one action was his undoing. The Department made enquiries and not only found that he had never had any of these jobs but he was not even Stephen Weinberg at all! His real name was Clifford Weyman, a hoaxer who had spent the war years in prison for helping men to dodge the draft into the U.S. Forces.

He not only lost his diplomatic post, but also his job as a radio reporter.

The Bogus Doctor

In Houston, Texas, Ben W. Jones saw an advertisement for a post as prison officer, and applied. He had, according to his references, had a distinguished career in many branches of the service. He was appointed.

The new prison officer was an outstanding success. His personality and methods, winning the confidence of the men, organizing clubs, classes and sporting activities, brought him to the notice of the authorities, and he was appointed to one of the most difficult and responsible jobs in the whole service. This was at the Huntsville prison which housed some of the toughest criminals in the whole state. Here too he gained the co-operation of the prisoners and set up a variety of novel social activities.

Things went well until one day a prisoner reading a magazine discovered that the respected officer Ben W. Jones was no more than a confidence man with a long string of aliases behind him.

Soon the whole story was out. Ben W. Jones was really Ferdinand Waldo Demara, a man who had deserted from both the U.S. Army and Navy. As Dr. Robert Linton French he had joined a Trappist monastery in Kentucky and then left, having broken his vows and stolen food. In 1952 as Dr. St. Cyr he had become a surgeon in the Royal Canadian Navy, performing operations, extracting bullets from men wounded in Korea. On one occasion he deftly removed a tooth from the jaw of his commanding officer.

The publication of the details of Dr. St. Cyr's brilliant military record had come to the notice of the real Dr. St. Cyr as well as of a Dr. Hamann whom he had previously impersonated, and a naval enquiry board that had discharged him from the service and ordered him to leave Canada.

This was what had eventually brought him to Texas after having sold his story to a newspaper and made a sort of living wandering from town to town.

On the discovery of his many impersonations he was called to the office of the prison governor and asked to deny that he was the man mentioned in the article. He did so, accusing his fellow officers of taking the word of a prisoner before his, and he challenged anybody who did so to a duel.

The duel was never fought. Instead, Jones—St. Cyr—Hamann—Demara packed up his belongings and left.

The head of the Texas Department of Correction admitted that it had lost one of the best of its officers, and stated that if Demara could come back with the right qualifications and references the Department would gladly take him back into service.

Why did such a brilliant and able man become an arch-imposter? Why had he not worked to obtain genuine qualifications? When asked he replied, "Rascality, pure rascality."

He continued his life in a new career, this time as a genuinely ordained minister of the church.

The Home-Grabbers

The career of Andrew James Spence was much more sordid. Under a score or more names he had been a crocodile hide exporter, cybernetics expert, computerized marriage counsellor, doctor of divinity, doctor of medicine, orange juice concentrate king, lumber tycoon, arms smuggler, dentist, Texas industrialist, rabbi, process server, and sex change consultant.

He is generally regarded by those who know him as one of the greatest confidence tricksters in history, and that is saying a great deal. He describes himself as a third generation bastard. His sphere of occupation covers the world from Addis Ababa to Alaska and he seems to be capable of turning up anywhere. The police are barely able to keep up with him, and when they do their main object appears to be to encourage him to go elsewhere.

Up to 1977 he was "business manager" for a certain Dr. John Brown whose ambition was to make San Francisco the sex change capital of the world—or so he said. Spence's job was to solicit business, to look for those who would pay up to $5,000 for the operation. The business ended in 1977.

Another of his exploits was to apply to the State Energy Commission for a $2 million grant to assist in the establishment of an Energy Conservation Corps. When it was turned down, he complained of rudeness on the part of the Commission staff.

In March 1978, Mr. Robert Lueck of Berkeley, California, advertised in the East Bay Tri-Valley News for a retired couple to live in with his semi-invalid mother at her home in Orinda. Spence and his wife Jane answered the advertisement stating that they had expert knowledge of nutrition and home care, and for years had been engaged in paramedical work. At first they occupied a single rear room, but before long they had taken possession of the whole house, and Spence had turned the best room into his office, controlling the staff and changing everything round to suit his own and his wife's convenience.

Anxious about strangers taking over the premises and about the treatment of his mother, Lueck went to the police. When they arrived at the house Spence told them that he had a perfect right to live there and showed them an agreement according to which the old lady had given them the right, even up to 100 days after her death. The police had to advise Lueck to leave the house, for there was no more he could do. He left, taking his mother with him.

Meanwhile Spence and his wife had been to the administrators of Mrs. Lueck's house and demanded of them $3000 for "damage to their professional reputations," and the right to live there permanently.

Lueck's next desperate move was to break into the house by night at a time when he knew they were out. When he went through their papers he found files full of malpractice suits in Jane Spence's name against various doctors. Among the papers was a newspaper story about Spence's career as a sex-change expert and many others detailing former frauds. It was lucky that Spence, like many other con-men, could not resist keeping records of his own sordid triumphs.

From there Lueck went to the bank and to the District Attorney and told the whole story, with a demand that the pair should be got out of the house immediately.

No eviction was necessary, for Spence and his wife knew that the game was up. While the authorities were considering what to do the couple decamped by night. They left behind only a cup of marijuana seeds in the kitchen and a few scraps of paper sketching their plans for altering the premises including a project for a mushroom garden cultivated by ex-convicts.

By that time the Spences were far away but Mrs. Lueck dared not live in the house for more than two days at a time for fear they would return. A few days after they departed Lueck received a telegram from them saying that they were going to sue him for "breach of contract and other damages."

The cost of sending the telegram was charged to the receiver.

Tragic Young Genius

In the 18th century the interests of the English gentry began to spill over into the realms of literature and art. This was the age of the Grand Tour in which they sent their sons to finish their education with a journey of six months or more to the principal cultural places in France and Italy, from which countries they brought home books, manuscripts, pictures, pottery, statuettes, and other antiquities to stock their family libraries and museums.

In Britain there was little original classical art, but there existed a profusion of legends, poems and chronicles from Anglo-Saxon times onward, and a newly-discovered manuscript could command a high price from a collector besides bringing fame to the discoverer. Here, then, was a comparatively unexplored field for the literary forger.

The most famous of these was the 17-year-old Thomas Chatterton, born in 1752 in Bristol. He was the son of a rather eccentric schoolmaster and from his earliest years was an avid reader, delighting in anything that smacked of antiquity. He would remain in his little attic reading his books and cherished parchments saved from the muniment room of the Church of St. Mary Redcliffe, and writing stories of medieval heroes and heroines.

Before he was 15 he was already "discovering" ancient manuscripts; some he said were from the parish chest, others supposed to have been sent to him by correspondents. Many of these were poems and dramatic fragments of rare merit which it was inconceivable could have been written by a mere boy. Chatterton was soon faced with only two choices, first to confess that he had written them himself, the second to produce more and more, continuing the deception. He chose the latter.

Working as an attorney's clerk, he went on writing in his spare time, and was only 16 when he sent to a London publisher "copies of several ancient poems and an interlude . . . wrote by one Rowley, a priest in Bristol who lived in the reigns of Henry VI and Edward IV." These being unacknowledged, he wrote to the author and critic Horace Walpole, sending other "ancient" verses. Walpole's advice to the boy to stick to the attorney's office until he had made a fortune, had no effect. His master the attorney, tired of his waywardness, cancelled his indentures and in April, 1770, Chatterton arrived in London to pursue his chosen career of poet, literary man and forger.

Here he wrote and wrote, seeming to be able to produce at will prose in the style of almost any author. Political letters, eclogues, lyrics, operas and satires flowed from his pen. His work was usually accepted but payment arrived late or never. His "discovery," Rowley's *Excelente Balade of Charitie*, was sent to a publisher and rejected.

At the beginning of July, 1770, he moved from Shoreditch to a tiny chamber in Brook Street, Holborn. Between May and August his total earnings came to £4-15-9d (about $20). He was starving, even eating mouldy bread, when he could get it. He was refused further credit at the bread shop but he was still proud and obstinate. His landlady offered to return the rent he had paid but he angrily refused to take it.

On 23rd August he was found in his attic dead from arsenic poisoning. He left behind twelve lines of rhyme which ended:

"Have mercy, Heaven! When here I cease to live,
And this last act of wretchedness forgive."

He was 17 years and 9 months old. The usual verdict of unsound mind was returned at the Coroner's inquest.

For years controversy raged as to whether the Rowley manuscript was genuine. Dr. Samuel Johnson visited Bristol six years after the boy's death, saw them, but was convinced they were forgeries. "This is the most extraordinary young man that has encountered my knowledge," he said. "It is wonderful how the whelp has written such things."

In the death of Chatterton, England lost one who might have become one of its greatest literary figures.

Shakespeare Rediscovered

Chatterton's literary works have given him a secure place among English poets. Those of William Ireland who, when he was also 17, wrote a complete play and passed it off as one of Shakespeare's, was not. The hoax perpetrated on the London dramatists and theatregoers was, however, much more spectacular than anything Chatterton ever did.

As the son of a London engraver and dealer in rare books,

Ireland became acquainted as a boy with the old English script and dreamed that one day he would himself produce a great literary work. In 1794 his father took him to Stratford-on-Avon where he was deeply moved at seeing the place where Shakespeare had spent his youth. He might not have thought of forgery had he not met a local poet named John Jordan who had published many Shakespearean stories and had even forged the will of John, the poet's father.

Seeing this and his father's credulous interest in it, he conceived the idea of himself forging ancient documents. He began by first copying Shakespeare's style and handwriting, then produced leases, contracts with actors, notes and receipts. He even composed a love-letter from Shakespeare to Anne Hathaway enclosing a lock of hair. For all these he used paper taken from Elizabethan folios and ink which had all the signs of age.

He explained to his father that a rich man, knowing how interested he was in anything having to do with Shakespeare, had given him these because they had originally been bequeathed by the poet to one of the boy's ancestors, William Henry Irelaund, who had saved him from drowning.

It was a tall story, but his father and many scholars who might have been more suspicious, believed it. Even Boswell, Dr. Johnson's biographer, who had already had experience of the Chatterton affair, was taken in. When he saw the bogus relics he knelt before them saying, "I now kiss the invaluable relics of our Bard, and thanks to God that I have lived to see them."

In a moment of rashness young Ireland mentioned to some of his admiring visitors that he had actually discovered a new and complete Shakespeare play. From then on his father, credulous as ever, kept on pestering him to see it. He, knowing nothing about the length and construction of a Shakespeare play, was now faced with the formidable task, not only of writing it, but of writing it in Shakespeare's own hand. It was quite beyond him. Instead, at the end of two months he showed his father a play, *Vortigern and Rowena*, which was one he said he had copied from the original. Had his father been less enthusiastic and more cynical he would have realized that the idea had come from a large picture which hung over the chimney-piece in the study.

The dramatic world, though not quite as enthusiastic, did not question the play's authenticity, and the playwright Sheridan bought it for £300. The love story of Vortigern, Prince of Britain, and Rowena, a daughter of Hengist the Saxon leader, was produced at Drury Lane in April, 1796, to a full house with a member of the famed Kemble family in the name part.

It was evident almost from the start that this was not true Shakespeare. The sentiment was false, the language and composition mediocre. Not even the best acting could hide the glaring faults. Kemble made the best of it. He knew, and the house knew, that it was a fake. When he came to the lines in which he addressed Death—

"And with rude laughter and fantastic tricks,
Thou clapp'st thy rattling fingers to thy sides,"

his voice rose to a climax and, glaring meaningfully at the audience, enunciated the next line—

"And when this solemn mockery is o'er—"

There was a tumult in the pit which lasted a full ten minutes, then Kemble, taking the house into his confidence, with irony in his powerful voice, repeated the line.

It was the end, the one and only night. Ireland, shamed, confessed all his forgeries. Kemble said that it was a pity the play could not have been performed on the 1st of April instead of the 2nd. Even then Ireland's father refused to believe that all his son's writings were no more than forgeries.

The young man was neither tried nor imprisoned. Doggedly he went on writing play after play, several novels and a good deal of inferior poetry until his death in 1835. None of it warrants a place in literary history.

As curios and mementoes of that strange evening in Drury Lane Theatre his Shakespearean efforts are now on show in the British Museum.

The Counterfeiters

The dictionary definition of the word "counterfeit" is, to make an imitation without authority for the purpose of defrauding. The word is particularly used in connection with the making of imitation money. At first it applied to coinage and included such offences as filing, clipping and gilding as well as making facsimile copies. It was difficult to detect and even more difficult to track down once the coins had been "uttered" or circulated. Hardly a week passed in centuries past without some news-sheet or other producing reports of the circulation of false coins, and occasionally of the arrest of counterfeiters.

During the 20th century in most countries notes have taken the place of coins of higher value, and counterfeiting has been more concerned with printing than with anything else. But with more modern and sophisticated methods of note-printing and detection, the counterfeiter is often a petty criminal concerned with the copying and circulation of smaller items such as vouchers and tickets.

One of the most bizarre exploits in currency fraud occurred in 1924 and concerned the Bank of Portugal and the British firm of Waterlow and Sons, who were unwittingly drawn into the fraud.

The principal was Virgilio Alves Reis, a Portuguese colonial official. His plan was to double the circulation of certain Portuguese banknotes—2,000 of them—by having the counterfeit notes, if such they could be called, printed by the same firm that had made the originals, and *from the same plates.*

It was most ingenious. First he had to choose the confederates who would fit in perfectly. The only one to know the whole scheme from the beginning was Gustav Hennies, a German businessman. Of the other two, both at the outset completely innocent, one was José Bandiera, brother of the Portuguese Minister at The Hague and the other Karel Marang van Ysselveera, a Dutch merchant acting as Consul-General of Persia at The Hague and as such, enjoying diplomatic immunity from search. Both had the right contacts and privileges.

Reis began by showing the other three a forged contract bearing official signatures for the arrangement of a loan for Angola, then a Portuguese possession. The money was to be sent in banknotes which were to be printed by Waterlow, the official printers of notes to the Portuguese Government. Negotiations were to be conducted by van Ysselveera, who went to London bearing a letter of introduction from Bandiera's brother the Minister.

The printing of the notes was to be a purely Portuguese affair and was to be kept secret owing to the political upheavals which could be feared if an announcement was premature. Sir William Waterlow agreed, and some weeks later received forged letters and contracts purporting to be from the Governor of the Bank of Portugal, the High Commissioner for Angola and many prominent bankers. The notes were to be printed from the plates already used—in other words they would be duplicates of those already in circulation, but once they arrived at their destination they would all be overprinted with the word ANGOLA.

In due course van Ysselveera received them and took them under diplomatic cover to Lisbon. With them the conspirators bought foreign currency, shares, etc. Only gradually it dawned on Portuguese officials, bankers and merchants what was happening as more and more 500-escudo notes appeared in circulation, some being exact duplicates of the numbers in use. The investigation raised suspicions that the irregularity had to do with the Bank of Angola and Metropole recently founded by Reis and his colleagues. When the offices of its Oporto branch were raided, the evidence, in bundles of new notes, was discovered.

Hennies fled to Germany; van Ysselveera was tried in Holland and received only eleven months for receiving stolen property. Reis produced more forged documents allegedly implicating the Governor and some directors of the Bank of Portugal. This delayed his trial for five years, but in 1930 both he and Bandiera were found guilty and imprisoned for 20 years each.

An Ill-Defined Boundary

Where does legal transcription or representation pass into the illegal? The boundary is well enough marked in currency cases; in literature, drama and music, the limits are defined by the laws of copyright. In art and sculpture, because of their nature the situation is not so clear.

There is, however, one branch, the deliberate copying of old masters and period pieces where it can be made if frauds can be detected. Alceo Dossena, a restorer of broken statues, found ways of simulating antique materials—dipping marble into acid to give it the appearance of wear, and using paint soaked off old statues and picture frames to put an antique look on wood. In this way he created work which deceived the greatest experts. A 14th century Madonna and Child and a marble Athena bought for $120,000, both made by him, were exhibited in the Cleveland Museum of Art. When he confessed to having created pieces attributed to medieval and ancient sculptors even the experts at first refused to believe him.

In 1918 the Metropolitan Museum of Art, New York, bought for $40,000 a 7-foot-tall statue of an Etruscan warrior dating, it was believed, from the early years of the Roman Republic in the 5th century B.C. It has in fact been made by a family team of Italian sculptors named Riccardi who had constructed the figure, painted and glazed it, then smashed it to bits and laboriously pieced the fragments together again so as to make authentic marks on it. It had remained in the Museum for 15 years before any fraud was suspected, and another 22 before a thorough enquiry was made. Then it was found that the paints contained manganese, a substance which the ancient Etruscans could never have used.

This was only one of the pieces the family made. Others were a two-horse chariot acquired by the British Museum in 1912, another figure called the Old Warrior, and a huge head with helmet 4 feet 7 inches high were both sold to the Metropolitan Museum.

Even after the most detailed examinations, many experts could not believe that the statues were fakes. It was only when, on 5th January, 1960, one of the family aged 75 who had helped to make them, produced out of his pocket a left thumb which he said was the one missing from the hand of the Old Warrior, that they had doubts. When the thumb was put to the statue's hand it was a perfect fit. He had kept the thumb as a souvenir for more than 40 years.

In 1971, the congregation of the Marienkirche in Lübeck, West Germany, were celebrating 700 years of the church's existence and had engaged Dietrich Fey, head of a firm of art restorers to make good the medieval frescoes which had been damaged and almost effaced in 1942 when a bomb had destroyed the roof and damaged the nave. The Government had given some £20,000 ($56,000) towards the restoration, and when complete and unveiled the frescoes were regarded as such a valuable masterpiece that they were portrayed on postage stamps.

For all this Dietrich Fey obtained the credit and most of the profits until one of the craftsmen, Lothar Malskat, inspired mainly by the desire to have at least part of the credit if not his share of the cash, announced that the "restorations" were his work, that all were fakes and that among the inspirations for the saints and holy figures were photographs of such people as Marlene Dietrich, Rasputin, and pictures of the Mongol tyrant Genghis Khan.

A lawsuit and an enquiry followed in which Malskat's assertions were proved. He was sentenced to 18 months' imprisonment and his employer Dietrich Fey, who had been behind the frauds, to 20 months.

To What End?

Field-Marshal Hermann Goering was an avid collector of masterpieces who at the Nuremberg trials was found guilty of war crimes. When his collection was examined, one of the 1200 paintings, *The Woman Taken in Adultery*, turned out to be a hitherto unknown Vermeer and, as there were only 36 other known paintings by this artist, the discovery of a 37th was something of an event. When an enquiry was made as to its origin it was found that Goering's agent had paid £150,000 ($600,000) for it to "someone in Amsterdam" in forged banknotes.

Who had committed this, which in Dutch eyes was an act of collaboration? A long sequence of enquiries led the investigators to a night-club owner named Han van Meegeren. He was arrested and, after three weeks of questioning including threats of execution, he made the astonishing confession that the painting was not a Vermeer at all but that he had painted it himself in the style of Vermeer. Moreover, it was only one of a number he had done and passed off as Old Masters.

The sensation rocked the art world. Van Meegeren confessed to having forged 14 Dutch masterpieces which had gone to various art collections. The experts refused to believe him and challenged him to paint the picture again without reference to the original. Instead, under constant supervision of witnesses and in a locked room in the local gaol, he produced a picture of Christ teaching in the temple—the last he was ever to paint. The experts were confounded and reputations crashed.

It turned out that this man had at one time been a rising young artist of whom an art critic had demanded a bribe in exchange for writing a review praising his work, and he had refused to pay. From then on everything he did had been condemned and, as an act of revenge on the whole art world, he had produced these forgeries, all with forged signatures.

In 1947 he was tried and found guilty, not of collaboration, but of forging signatures. He was sentenced to a year's imprisonment but before the sentence could be begun, he had died of a heart attack.

More recently the British public has been thrilled at the audacious way in which the critics have been fooled by a former painter and decorator turned artist named Tom Keating. Thirteen of his drawings had been attributed to the English landscape artist, Samuel Palmer; some of them had gone into art galleries at a cost of thousands of pounds.

When the story came out, Keating told astonished reporters that he had faked more than two thousand pictures—how many he was not sure—in the styles of scores of painters. Some he had done as a joke and he had given away more than he had sold. Sometimes he would do three or four in an afternoon.

He was quite open about it all. He had no idea where they all were, and he had done so many that he himself could not tell in some cases which were his and which not. In the story of his life published in 1977 there is a chapter, very honestly written on *The Gentle Art Of Sexton Blaking* (faking) in which he says:

> "I have never made a secret of my ability to make fakes; I have boasted about it in pubs and at dinner parties. I've told almost everyone I've ever met about them. The only thing that amazes me is that I wasn't exposed in the press a lot sooner."

The book contains the whole amazing story of the Palmer fakes and an appendix in which is a list of some 130 artists whose style he has imitated and of the fakes he knows he has made. There are, he says, probably many more than appear in the appendix.

Which leaves us with the question, "What is a masterpiece? and why is it so much superior to the fake, if the best experts have so much difficulty in telling them apart?" But this is a question not to be answered here.

One postscript, in August, 1978. It has now been revealed after a century and a half that a painting attributed to John Constable was not by John at all but by his son Lionel. Curiouser and curiouser!

It is becoming more and more difficult to make sure that a painting in a gallery is really what it is said to be. The situation is now such that, in the words of a BBC commentator, "Attribution of paintings is one of the light industries of the art world."

BIZARRE CRIMES

The Thief and the Resurrection Man
Does Money Always Matter?
"Set a Thief . . ."
Grass
Pay-Off Number Thirteen
How to Stop a Nagging Wife
The Hijackers
Grievous Bodily Harm
The Young Poisoner
Paw Marks in the Cement
Punishment to Fit the Crime

BIZARRE CRIMES

The Thief and the Resurrection Man

Everything has a value to somebody. Thieves taking a van clear out a house, robbing it of everything moveable—cabinets, piano, radio, carpets, clothing, trinkets, jewels—the lot. Then they go for the fixtures, switch off the electricity at the meter box, take away cable and plugs, chandeliers, reading lamps, freezers and refrigerator; they disconnect the gas supply, remove the cooker; they turn off the water, tear the copper piping from the wall, even remove cisterns and lavatory chains.

The family returns to the house to find it no more than an empty shell.

What about the people in the next house? Didn't they see what was going on?

They may have, but really it was none of their business. Besides they weren't too friendly with the folks next door. They just thought it might be a normal moving-out.

All this has happened.

Everything has a value to somebody. The vicar is called up by the church caretaker on a wet Sunday morning. The rain is pouring through the roof onto the altar and the chancel carpet is soaked. There are pools in the nave and along the aisles, and the pews are too wet to be used. Thieves have stolen the lead from the roof.

All this has happened.

Even prisons are not exempt from this type of theft. On the morning that Britton Batley walked out of a prison in Manchester, England, after serving a three-year sentence he was met by a truck driven by one of his mates "outside." Some hours later the same truck was stopped by police. It was found to have been loaded with five hundredweights (560 lbs.) of copper belonging to the prison authorities.

Theft is a crime dating from the beginning of human history, ages and ages before Jacob stole Esau's birthright. When Henry VIII's commissioners despoiled the monasteries they too committed thefts. The only difference was that they had the law—Henry's law—on their side.

In Queens, a borough of New York City, a group of teenagers broke into graves in order, the police said, to sell the skulls of the dead to a self-styled warlock or male witch. In early 1977 a famous grave was despoiled by robbers in Switzerland and Sir Charles Chaplin's body was removed, not for purposes of casting spells or making sorcery, but for ransom.

There is nothing new about grave-robbing, for in England 150 years ago not just the skulls but whole corpses were needed by the schools of anatomy for dissection. Since at that time the law allowed them to have only the bodies of murderers for this purpose, the supply ran far short of the demand.

Hence the body-snatchers or resurrection men, as they were called. The Home Office authorities, knowing how necessary it was that students should know the details of the human body, instructed the police not to interfere with them more than was necessary. As long as only newly-buried paupers were taken, the authorities characteristically did not worry much about it, but soon the body-snatcher became a menace, taking the remains of the wealthier classes, rifling the graves and often not even taking the trouble to fill them in. Churchwardens and the families of the bereaved often had to post armed men in the churchyards by night to prevent this kind of desecration. The corpses of the well-to-do were sometimes buried in iron coffins, and graves were protected by cage-like iron bars called *mort-safes*. So scarce did the supply of human remains become that the price per corpse rose round about 1828 from the former £2 ($4) to a maximum of £14 ($30). An import business developed (though it probably never entered the Trade Statistics) and both English students of anatomy and their teachers went to Paris where they could get bodies for as little as 7 francs each.

Much more gruesome even than this was the body-cutter who purchased the body from the resurrection man and cut it up for sale in the same way as one would the carcass of a sheep, pig, calf or ox. Moreover, whereas in 1828 it was a felony punishable by death to steal the carcass of an animal and by transportation to receive such a carcass, it was no more than a misdemeanour punishable by fine or imprisonment to buy and cut up a human body. Scoundrels like William Burke and William Hare solved the problem by manufacturing their own dead bodies. They added murder to the crime of body-snatching when in Edinburgh they made a practice of enticing men to their lodgings and then drugging and suffocating them in order to sell their dead bodies. Hare turned King's evidence and Burke was hanged. It was this gruesome state of affairs that brought about the Anatomy Act of 1832 stating the conditions under which bodies might be had and by what procedures.

That was the end of the resurrection man.

Does Money Always Matter?

Petty larceny is well-known and indeed common among all of us, often without our being conscious of it. Technically the office worker who walks off with as little as a paper clip is guilty, trifling though this offence may be. But, should he allow himself more licence, from paper clips he may extend his activities to account books, then to typewriters and copying machines. In the machine shop it may start with a simple screw or a packet of screws, from that to the wrench, then to the whole tool kit. Is there a line to be drawn or is it a matter of degree?

Mohammed Bikhtani had not one scruple. From Isfahan

University in Iran he stole 295 tables, 340 typewriters, 959 rolltop desks, 1069 chairs and 27,056 paper clips. One wonders how in the world he got away with it and how much equipment was left after he had finished. When charged he put forward a novel plea. He claimed that the thefts were in no way aimed at personal gain, but that they were all parts of a serious academic exercise. What the object was, the report does not say. He went to prison, but on his release the value of this "academic exercise" seems to have paid off. He was made Professor of Criminology at the same university.

If Bikhtani's plea was a sound one it seems to bear out the assertion that one does not always rob for money. Louis Giraud, a French student 18 years of age, marched one day into the bank on the Avenue du Pardo in Marseilles and held up the manager and staff. When a customer grabbed him from the back, the resistance he put up was negligible, and he was taken like a lamb to the Sureté.

Later, called before the judge and threatened with an examination by a psychiatrist, he protested that he was perfectly sane.

"Please, sir," he pleaded, "all I want is to go to gaol so that I will have time and a place to study."

He didn't get it, for the prison was already more than full.

Admittedly, people will steal for the most bizarre reasons. Shoichi Fujita of Kobe in Japan left the store in which he had been shopping with two cream buns that had not been paid for. When stopped and searched he was found to have three million yen taped to his stomach. He was too thrifty to pay for anything if it could be avoided. "I have been saving for years," he said, "and I have found that the best way to do it is not to spend."

Shoppers in an English supermarket were concerned when a lady in a large flowered hat fainted at the checkout. On removing her hat to make her comfortable they discovered she had been carrying two stolen frozen chickens in it. The cold temperature had affected the supply of blood to her brain and this had been the cause of her swoon.

Whatever happens to be around in plenty, especially if access is easy, is fair game for the thief. Coffee in Brazil, church ornaments and works of art in Italy, diamonds in Hatton Garden, bottles of wine in France, rolls of cloth in Yorkshire, tobacco, cigarettes and motor cars everywhere.

California produces tons upon tons of seedless raisins. When they began to disappear from processing plants in the Fresno district, the blame was laid on gangs of rustlers. According to Detective Don Hard of the Fresno Sheriff's Office, thieves even used the forklift truck belonging to one grower to put a pair of one-ton bins on to their own truck, then drove off. They sold their haul to unsuspecting packers who bought the fruit in good faith for $840 a ton—net profit $1,680 (£900).

Perhaps the most cavalier theft however, took place in 1978 in France. Police patrolling the road late at night stopped a young man who was driving his young lady home in a mechanical digger. It turned out that the digger was stolen, but the man vigorously protested his innocence explaining that the digger was a wedding present from some friends and he was on his honeymoon. What's more the story was true—only sadly his friends had indeed neglected to pay for their generous gift!

Set a Thief

Few cars are safe from being illegally driven off. Thousands disappear in London alone within a year, some to be used for other crimes, some to be hastily re-vamped and re-sprayed, then exported to the Continent. The same happens all over the world, especially in the United States, where cars are stolen to order. It is, with the right contacts, possible to specify the make and model of the car you want *in advance* of its being stolen!

One of the grand masters in the art of car theft in the United States is 30-year-old James Anthoni. He admits that he has master-minded the theft of nearly 3,000 cars in ten years without ever being arrested. In one year alone his profits were between $60,000 and $70,000.

He entered the profession immediately after leaving high school when a man offered him his first job stealing cars. He was eventually given $200 for every one he drove off, and managed to make that sum each week—good pay for a short time working on the job.

"It was really quite simple," he said. "First I contacted people in the auto business. Then I'd get duplicate keys from the dealers.

"In exchange for $15 to $75 they would give me the code numbers and I'd have the keys made. To avoid trouble I'd bribe the cop on the beat. Once I had to give a sergeant $2,000, but that was because fifteen stolen cars were involved."

His biggest sale was $3,000 for a Winnebago motor home, whose retail value at the time was about $16,000.

After a few years in the trade he reached a point where he believed gambler's odds were rising against him and wisely he decided to quit. So he simply gave himself up to the police, told them almost everything he had done, testified against several men in the car theft rings and was forthwith granted immunity from arrest.

That was in 1976. Ten or more years in the business had made him an expert not only in the theft of vehicles, but also in preventing it. He went on television, discussed his past and talked to insurance companies.

In January, 1978, he was on hand at the Greater New York Automobile Show displaying the latest anti-thief devices. He admitted that he still had some of the profits from his illegal ventures.

Some car thieves have not been so lucky. In Liverpool, England, one day in August, 1978, an off-duty constable went into a shop with his wife. When he returned ten minutes later to get his car it was no longer there.

A big police hunt was mounted around Liverpool and the car was found only a street or two away from the store. It appeared that the thief had seen only too late that he had company in the car—the police constable's baby.

Not every anti-thief device is as efficient a burglar alarm as a newly-awakened baby. A youth in San Carlos, Arizona, found himself in court in March, 1978, for manufacturing his own anti-theft device. Unfortunately for him he had forgotten to disconnect it before he started the car. When he turned on the ignition in front of his home the 6-inch incendiary device under the car blew up. He was thrown away from the car into the roadway; the car burst into flames and was completely destroyed.

Police investigators were quickly on the scene, for the youth, whose name was withheld for security reasons, had given undercover information about drug trafficking that had led to the arrest of seven suspected pushers. They thought this might have been a device planted in the youth's car as a revenge for his squealing.

It was not so. Now he faced charges for its illegal manufacture.

Grass

Do we all know what grows in our gardens?

Mr. Fred Kechter was surprised and delighted to see a plant which he had not put there, springing up vigorously in his flowerbed. It looked good, it did well and soon became his pet. Proudly he showed it off to everyone and the local newspaper reporter got to know about it.

One day the reporter brought a photographer with him to Fred's house and a picture was taken of him standing proudly by the side of his wonderful 12-foot-high foundling.

The day after the photograph appeared in the newspaper Fred received a visit from the police who politely asked him to accompany them to the station. The plant was *Cannabis Sativa*—Indian hemp or marijuana—which had apparently grown from bird seed accidentally scattered there.

So, bird-fanciers, beware!

John Mills, aged 24, had a farm in Mason County, Washington, where he, quite illegally, grew the cannabis plant. One day the sheriff's deputy called at his place, confiscated his whole crop and arrested him on a drug charge. But Judge Frank Baker, before whom he was brought, was evidently a man of advanced views. He ordered Mills to circle the courthouse twenty times on four successive Sunday mornings wheeling a barrow full of dirt on which was one marijuana plant and a sign reading "Decriminalize Marijuana!"

Pay-Off Number Thirteen

Twenty-three-year-old David Hargis was a marine drill instructor in San Diego, California. He was handsome, popular, a good officer with the cadets, well-liked by his buddies—and married.

But all wasn't well. Somehow his pay could never be made to cover his expenses and he had run into debt. Even though he had recently re-enlisted to get extra salary, his credit payments were still behind.

David's wife Carol was thirteen years older than he was. At 36, she thought, one ought to be sitting back to enjoy the good life, not limping along with a load of debt on one's back. Besides, Carol was already involved with a local bartender. She had begun to think that if David could be got out of the way she would be free, she would not be liable for any of the family's debts and what was more, she would be able to draw $20,000 life insurance from her husband's policy.

Here was a situation with all the ingredients of a first-class murder if it could be done cleverly. But Carol was neither clever nor keen to do the job herself, so she called in the aid of the woman next door who was far more unscrupulous than she was. The price offered to Mary Depew was $1,000, which was turned down, and the bargain had ultimately to be concluded to divide the insurance on a fifty-fifty basis. If David's death could be contrived to appear accidental, they would be able to draw double the pay-off and end up with $20,000 each.

The problem was, how to arrange the "accident." Their first scheme was for Mary Depew to run her car into David as he left the Hargis apartment on foot, but they soon found it could hardly be done without incurring suspicion of evil intent and without risk of injury to the driver of the car.

So they thought again. It happened that David and Carol had a pet spider, a tarantula, which they kept locked up in a glass-fronted box or terrarium. The idea was to put it into David's bed, then when the police came to investigate his death Carol could say that the box had inadvertently been left open by one of the children.

That night they put the tarantula into the bed. Next morning David woke up as sprightly as ever. The tarantula was not one of the poisonous kind.

Still, tarantula poison appeared to be the best idea they had so far hit on, so Mary got another tarantula, cut it open and removed the venom sac which Carol put into a blackberry pie. When the pie was brought to the table the place where the poison had been secreted was badly discoloured, and David wouldn't eat it.

The fourth idea was for Mary to crawl under David's truck, undo the brake-rods and anything else she could find. But when she tried, the job was too much for her. So Mary changed the plan. She brought some tabs of LSD for Carol to mix in French toast batter for David's breakfast. That morning he wasn't hungry, he felt a little off his feed and went off to work without eating anything at all.

They had to abandon plot six—to throw a small toaster from which the insulation had been removed into David's bathtub—too risky, so they hit on plan eight, to put bullets into the carburettor of his truck. This wouldn't work either, as they soon found out, nor would plans nine, ten and eleven which involved lye poisoning, stabbing and shooting. The possibility of "accidental" death seemed to be receding as the days passed.

Then Mary had a bright idea. An admitted junkie, she decided that the best way would be to kill him by shooting a bubble of air into his veins with a hypodermic syringe. Unfortunately for them the needle of the syringe broke before they had time to administer the injection.

So they fell back on plan twelve. David always drank beer before going to bed and they decided to poison it with a capsule. They did so, and three hours later they sneaked up to his bedroom expecting to see the worst—or best. David was lying there sleeping soundly and breathing as stentoriously as ever. When they examined the drink they found that the capsule hadn't disintegrated. Next morning David, innocent and cheerful as ever, came down to breakfast with a healthy appetite.

The thirteenth attempt was not even plotted. It was both straightforward and brutal. At one in the morning when both David and the children were asleep the two women stole up to his bedroom. Carol was shocked at the idea of bludgeoning him to death but Mary egged her on and, between them, the two killed him.

There was nothing clever about it, nothing that would give the idea that it had been accidental, everything that pointed to the two culprits—the wife and her friend. There was not a thing, as one newspaper report expressed it, that even Inspector Clouseau couldn't have handled. It was, for all the scheming that had gone before, a wide-open case. "I've never seen a murder botched so badly before," said the prosecuting counsel, "and their story was almost as dumb as their plot."

Both women received life sentences.

How to Stop a Nagging Wife

Janos Dey of Debreczen in north-west Hungary was a gentle sort of person but his wife was just the opposite. She never stopped talking—"Do this, do that!" He was utterly sick of being shoved hither and thither.

But he loved her dearly, that was the irony of it. He didn't want to rid himself of her presence but if, only *if* he could find some way of bringing her to her senses—if he could only see through the facade of the nagging wife the girl she once was before the storms began, he would be a happy man.

At last he had an idea—shock therapy. He would fake his own suicide. Surely that would provoke a flood of tenderness and shame that would last all her life.

He spent days putting together a protective harness which, while looking realistic would ease the pressure on his windpipe and jugular vein. Then one morning while his wife was out he eased himself into it and suspended himself, a convincing "corpse," from a beam in the ceiling of their bedroom.

His wife returned from her shopping, saw nobody downstairs, called. No answer. Then she went upstairs, saw the hanging figure, let out a piercing scream and fainted on the spot.

The woman next door, hearing the scream and wondering whatever was the matter, rushed across to find out. There was nobody downstairs. She called. No answer.

Was somebody ill? She went upstairs to find out and saw two figures, one hanging, dead, the other stretched out on the floor. Dead?

She didn't take the trouble to find out; that was a job for the police, but before fetching them, there was no harm in having a good look round, especially in the drawers and cupboards.

From the bedroom she took various small things, while all the time the hanging "corpse," quite conscious, knew everything that was going on. Then, as she passed him on the way to the bedroom door he seized the chance, made a supreme effort, twisted himself on the cord, lifted his foot and gave her a good kick behind.

She turned, saw the "corpse" swinging, screamed, dropped the loot and fell on the floor dead from a heart attack.

Dey managed to cut himself down; he revived his wife, summoned the police and gave himself up. Some time later he was charged with manslaughter and acquitted.

He told the court that his wife's nagging had stopped.

The Hijackers

Hijacking, especially of aircraft, is a comparatively recent crime, and examples of it are so frequently reported as to produce few surprises or bizarre episodes. The very first air hijack took place on June 16th, 1948, when a Cathay Pacific Airways flying-boat *Miss Macao* was seized by a gang of Chinese bandits led by a peasant named Wong-Yu Man shortly after taking off from Macao during a scheduled flight to Hong Kong.

The motive for the hijacking was to ransom the passengers, but the pilot resisted, the hijackers fired their weapons and the flying-boat crashed. The only survivor was the bandit leader Wong-Yu Man.

Although at first foul play was not suspected, after salvage teams had recovered the bullet-riddled fuselage, the police decided to place an informer in the bed next to Wong-Yu Man in the Hong Kong hospital. With the aid of a tape recorder the full story of the world's first aerial hijacking was pieced together from remarks made by the perpetrator to his fellow "patient."

One of the most recent and most bizarre of all hijackings ended on the evening of August 24th, 1978—with no sign of any hijacker and an embarrassed and bemused aircrew.

The 79 people aboard a TWA Boeing 707 had spent more than seven hours on the runway at Geneva as the clocks ticked round towards 5:30 p.m.—the time a bomb in the hold of the aircraft was supposed to explode.

Then, at 4 p.m., two Swiss officials gingerly climbed aboard, risking their lives, as they thought. Moments later they reappeared and all the passengers and crew followed them out of the plane unharmed.

Nobody knew who the hijacker was. If there had been one he seemed completely to have disappeared. Every piece of luggage was examined and every passenger questioned, but the Swiss police could not find the evidence they were looking for—one wig and one Groucho Marx moustache.

The false hair and bristle were last seen on a man who had stumbled along the darkened aisle of the plane as it passed over Ireland on the flight from New York. Few passengers took much notice for most of them had been engrossed in the in-flight film. When he reached the staff seats, the man dropped a bulky package onto the lap of a stewardess who was reading: "Give that to the captain," he said in English.

The stewardess sat still and carried on reading. The man nudged her. "Get going," he said.

The stewardess got going, and Groucho the hijacker slipped back into the shadows.

The package which was opened on the flight deck by the American captain, Robert Hamilton, might have provided the clue that the whole business was nothing more than an elaborate if dangerous hoax, for the hijacker's demands were bizarre to say the least, ranging right across any conceivable spectrum.

He demanded the release of Rudolf Hess from Spandau prison, the release of Sirhan Sirhan, Robert Kennedy's assassin, and the release of five Croatian liberationists.

The 17-page document, neatly typed but badly spelled began: "We, the Council of the Reciprocal Relief Alliance for Peace, Justice and Freedom everywhere and our organized armed officers, the United Revolutionary Soldiers, request your assistance to free His Excellency Rudolf Hess from the Spandau Prison."

The letter demanded that the plane be met at Geneva by a representative of the United States Armed Forces in Europe and suggested that the Commander in Europe, General Alexander Haig, should be informed. It added that there was a bomb on board due to explode at 5:30 p.m. There were even contingency plans for what would happen when the plane took off from Geneva complete with Hess, the five Croations and Sirhan Sirhan. The writer demanded parachutes and jump suits. He even specified the sizes.

The plane arrived in Geneva just before 8:30 a.m. and taxied to a halt on the runway. Armed guards took up positions in nearby buildings as the captain kept in touch with the airport operations room. There the plane remained until 4 p.m. when all concerned heaved a large sigh of relief as the passengers—including presumably Groucho without his disguise, got off.

What a mystery! Mrs. Mildred Meyer from Connecticut said, "I just wish I knew who it was on the plane but I couldn't see anybody who looked even remotely like a terrorist, and I had a pretty good look at everyone around me. I don't think anyone suspected me. I'm a little bit too old for that sort of thing."

"I'm sure that whoever did this," said TWA's International Vice President Stewart Long, "is some kind of nut, but what kind I don't know. It was almost like an Agatha Christie plot of trying to find the murderer."

The crew and passengers dispersed and the hoaxer has not been found to this day.

Talking about "nuts," an unnamed New Yorker, obviously a prize "nut" hijacked a policeman by jumping on his back and ordering him at knifepoint to walk with him to Cuba.

The policeman didn't raise any objection and calmly informed the hijacker that it could be done, but that it would involve three stops for refuelling. The hijacker fainted, dropped off the policeman who forthwith arrested him on an assault charge.

Grievous Bodily Harm

Rape is an unpleasant and normally highly unfunny crime which we usually associate with dark nights and ill-lit streets, but not so in Parramatta Gaol near Sydney, Australia. Among a group of entertainers visiting the prison to give a show was 23-year-old Sharon Hamilton, a singer of uplifting folk melodies.

She was singing *We Shall Overcome* when one of her male listeners, named Leonard Lawson, obviously himself overcome with emotion, leaped on to the stand and, holding a knife to Miss Hamilton's throat, told the audience to leave the room as he wanted to be alone with her.

This was obviously too much for the other prisoners who resented their entertainment being thus disturbed. They leaped on to the stand and overpowered Miss Hamilton's assailant.

More fortunate was the outcome of a case in Florida where two black citizens were sentenced to death for rape. When taken out of the cells for re-trial, witnesses were again called but the judge, Charles Scott, implied that their chances of acquittal were quite good, as the lady in question could no longer remember whether she had been raped or not!

Other strange assaults have occurred. Mr. Clarance Ramsay was one day standing outside his home in Houston, Texas, when a man came up to him and suddenly stabbed him in the back. Mr. Ramsay, wounded but still able to move, turned round to face his assailant and was astonished to hear him say, "Sorry, I thought you were somebody else."

It was a pity too that Mrs. Elizabeth McClelland ever left Belfast, Ulster, to live in Christchurch, New Zealand. Mrs. McClelland was an ardent advocate of the peace cause, and hoped by emigration to avoid the growing street violence that was going on in her home town.

Fate decreed otherwise. It so happened that there was a peace march in Christchurch and of course she had to be there, if only as an onlooker. She was caught in the crowd and was hit on the head with a peace march placard. She died in hospital later.

Wherever you may be, if it has your name on it . . .

The Young Poisoner

Graham Young was born in England in 1947. His mother had died when he was three months old and he was brought up by a stepmother whom he appeared to love very much indeed. A normal, chubby little boy, neither aggressive nor violent, he did well at school and passed the then universal 11-plus examination for entry to the local grammar school.

From early childhood he had been an avid reader and spent long periods in the local library. What his sister and friends did not know was that he had become fascinated by everything that had to do with poisons. He was soon collecting them. His family found out that he was carrying about with him such substances as acids and ether, and playing around with empty scent and varnish bottles.

Between the ages of 11 and 14 this fascination for poison and for reading about famous poisoners gripped him, and he began spending his weekly allowance at the chemists' shops, buying poisons and signing the poison book with assumed names. From the age of 10 his personality had begun to change. What had been a quiet, obedient and affectionate child turned into an aggressive, argumentative, self-willed and thoroughly unpleasant youth.

He became interested in black magic; little clay images pierced with pins were found in his room. He was obsessed with stories about Adolf Hitler and the Nazis, even went about wearing a home-made armband on which the swastika had been drawn.

It was round about this time, when he was 12, that members

of his family developed illnesses, revealing symptoms varying from stomach and abdominal pains to muscular weakness and tremors. The young lad was already putting such poisons as belladonna and antimony potassium tartrate into his family's food and drink. When his sister accused him after one episode in which her tea had been poisoned with belladonna, he denied that he had had anything to do with it and went to bed in tears. She was so deeply moved by his reaction that she apologized.

He was by this time callously experimenting on his own family and friends to see what the effects were of his chosen poisons. His best school friend had to be taken to hospital; his stepmother became gradually weaker and weaker until she died. The boy afterwards confessed that he had put 20 grains of thallium into the cake she ate on the night before her death. Then his father became ill. The doctors were baffled, suspecting Mr. Young of attempted suicide following on his wife's death.

The events leading to Graham Young's arrest started at school. He had been taking poisons to the science laboratory for analysis and among the things his science master had seen were technical books on the subject, portraits of famous poisoners, short poems composed by him on the virtues of the substances he used. And finally came the mysterious illness of Graham's school friend Williams.

The science master revealed his suspicions to the Head; the Head got in touch with the family doctor; a psychiatrist was called in and he was struck with the boy's detailed knowledge. His self-confidence betrayed him. The police were notified; they called at his home, found the bottles of antimony and later discovered more than one cache of poisons in various out-of-the-way places.

At the trial the court was convinced that the boy was completely devoid of moral sense, that although he knew the difference between right and wrong as seen by others, he had no power to follow the right course himself even had he wished, and, that if he remained free he would be likely to continue his experiments on family, friends and acquaintances. He was only 14 when, in July, 1962, he was sent to Broadmoor, a prison for mentally ill criminals, to serve 15 years.

He served $8\frac{1}{2}$ years. By 1970 it was considered that profound changes had taken place in his mental condition, though some of the staff at Broadmoor had grave doubts. He was granted parole for Christmas that year and was released on February 4th, 1971, aged 23. After a short period in a hostel in Slough he obtained a position as assistant storeman with a firm in Bovingdon, Hertfordshire, and took a bed-sitting room in Hemel Hempstead. The firm understood that he had recovered from a deep-seated personality disorder and had become completely normal.

Subsequent events showed how false this conclusion was. He had already while at Slough, bought thallium under an assumed name. One of the boys there had lost control of his leg muscles during a football game and this was followed by bouts of sickness which lasted for months. The ailment was diagnosed by the doctor as a urinary infection and treated as such. No suspicion had fallen on Graham Young while he was at the Slough hostel.

In May the terrible story of illness and death, this time in his workplace at Bovingdon, started again. First Bob Egle, the chief storeman, fell ill and died, then Fred Biggs, the packer. Among others who were affected by the poison he put into their drinks and their meals were driver Ron Hewitt, clerk Dave Tilson, his workmate Jethro Butt, and a woman worker Mrs. Smart. In November, a small team of doctors visited the firm to investigate the mysterious "Bovingdon Bug" as they called it, which was believed to be causing the epidemic of sickness raging among the staff.

The investigation ended with a meeting called mainly to reassure the workers that all the tests that had been done had failed to show anything in the factory or any of the processes carried on there that could have affected anybody's health. In that meeting Graham Young, careless and boastful, eager to show how much he knew, asked if the symptoms of those who had been ill were consistent with those of thallium poisoning. This, the worst thing he could do for himself, left the staff amazed at his intricate knowledge, but put the doctors on the track which led eventually to his conviction.

One day in November, the police called at the home of Graham Young's sister and asked where they could find him. She referred them to his father's residence, then in Sheerness. He was not there, but they traced him to the home of his aunt.

That was the end. In the interviews which followed, Young made a clean breast of everything, giving technical details of the effects of the poisons he had used. The remains of some of the victims were analyzed and sufficient evidence was produced to secure a conviction.

He was found guilty and imprisoned for life.

Paw Marks in the Cement

A street brawl, if the police are called in and the affair goes to court, may certainly be considered as a crime on somebody's part, if only a minor one. This story from Leeds, England, shows to what absurd extremes a simple act can lead.

A verse in the Book of Deuteronomy reads "Cursed be he that removeth his neighbour's landmark."

Mr. Rowley of Leeds, or rather his dog, certainly did that. The removal consisted of the defacement of a beautifully flat wet concrete forecourt with a line of paw marks. It happened in front of the shop belonging to the postmaster Mr. Bradbury.

"Grrr-h!" shouted Mr. Bradbury in a rage. "Gerroff!"

The dog did. Mr. Bradbury then took his trowel, gently worked away the dog's paw marks and re-created the shining smooth surface. No sooner had he done it and gone into the shop than the dog came back and made another line.

That started the trouble. Mr. Rowley, standing by, saw Mr. Bradbury throw a shovel at the dog, then run after it and aim a good kick.

Mr. Bradbury's toe landed on Mr. Rowley's shin.

Tempers rose to a white heat, eyes began to blaze. Fearing a fight, both Mrs. Bradbury and Mrs. Rowley, who had been attracted by the angry voices, ran towards the telephone box to call the police.

Mrs. Bradbury won, got into the box, grabbed the speaker.

Mrs. Rowley followed her, pulled her out of the box and both went down into the wet cement.

Now Mrs. Stevens, Mrs. Bradbury's aged mother, tried to get her daughter out, but Mrs. Rowley pulled her in too. Mr. Rowley, seeing what was happening to his wife, ran to her rescue. Mr. Bradbury stood in his way, tried to push him back and both rolled over into the cement beside the wives and the mother-in-law.

What the police found when they arrived might well have been seen on an old Keystone Komedy film.

Later in the magistrate's court the combatants were all dismissed with an injunction from his Worship to forget the whole business.

"Go not forth hastily to strive lest thou know not what to do when thy neighbour hath put thee to shame." (Proverbs 25.8.)

The forecourt in front of Mr. Bradbury's post office is now clean, flat and hard, with not a single paw mark on it.

Punishment to Fit the Crime

Can you commit a crime and yet be innocent? If innocence means ignorance of the fact, surely you can.

Mrs. Ivy Cannon was a cleaner in the British War Ministry who probably did not know when she covered her pots of home-made jam with "scrap" papers that she was using paper on which secret military information was printed. The crime, if such it was, cost her two years behind bars and a fine of £500 ($1,000).

Protected animals may also be considered state property. There is a certain kind of lobster native to Israeli-occupied southern Sinai which may not be caught. A Bedouin, Eid Umm Razik was picked up by officials of the Nature Preservation Society with a whole sackful of the protected crustaceans. When ordered to give them up, he resisted and attacked the officials. Later in court he was fined two camels for the offence and an additional one for assault.

Mr. Peter Howard, an English painter living in New Guinea,

was driving his car one day when by accident he killed a tribesman. When he was told by headmen of the tribe that he would have to pay £465 ($930) and four head of cattle in settlement he refused, so the family of the dead man went to his home and gave him a good thrashing. That made him change his mind. He paid the money and gave up the four head of cattle. Peace and goodwill restored, the tribe presented him in return with £10 ($20) and a pig.

Mrs. Farida Halim, an Arab woman on trial for theft, gave her judge a surprise. During the trial she gave birth to a baby and when asked to name it, she replied "Bara"—Not Guilty. The case was adjourned.

Prison is normally a grim place, but not in San Marino. This, the world's oldest and smallest republic, situated some 14 miles south-west of Rimini, is entirely surrounded by Italian territory. It is only 23 square miles in area and contains some 19,000 inhabitants. The town itself stands on the north end of a huge precipitous rock and La Rocca, the prison in which the imposter Cagliostro died in 1795, is a hilltop fortress from which nobody could escape even if he wanted. As it is, nobody seems to want to.

In 1977 the prison housed some 26 offenders from time to time, most of them cases of drunken driving. These are normally sentenced to a weekend in one of the six cells carved out of the wing of a converted monastery. More serious offenders are quickly released on parole. Recently Judge Emiliani ordered six youths to be given provisional liberty, the only conditions being that they could not leave San Marino territory, enter bars or restaurants or meet each other.

Today the prison has only two long-term occupants, Georgetti, a carpenter who murdered his wife and her sister, and Fantini, a plasterer who shot an old friend whom he caught in bed with his (Fantini's) mistress. They were convicted in 1975, but have yet to be sentenced by the independent judge from Rome who heard their case. They are expected to get about ten years each as there is no capital punishment in San Marino. With a good record they could be released immediately if they have already served five years.

But they are not at all anxious to be free. Their cells are kept unlocked all the time, they enjoy complete freedom within the prison, and are on familiar terms with the officers. They have television in the evening, the best of food and as much liquor as they can reasonably take. At first they were set to work within the prison itself, then they were given jobs outside under guard. Now they go off to work in the morning by themselves just like any other workmen and return "home" for the evening meal, earning 280,000 lire (about £180 or $360) a month each.

It is all part of the Council's re-education scheme. "Once Georgetti and Fantini were killers," says the judge. "Now they are honest, sensible people. We have monitored their progress and only gave them greater freedom when we knew they would respond. They have, and it's been a great success so far."

Neither prisoner is unhappy. "I miss my wife and family," says Fantini, "but we both went home for Christmas for three days and perhaps they will let us out more often from now on."

So far the only protesters are the relatives of their victims, but even they receive 20 per cent of the prisoners' pay.

BIZARRE ANIMALS

Stranger than Fiction
Virgin Birth
The Extra Senses of Animals
The Friendly Dolphin
Animals Outperform Humans
The Seahorse, a Pregnant Male
The Thorny Hedgehog
The Lemming's Death March
Powers of Endurance
The World of the Grasshopper
Freaks of Nature
Breeding for Use and Fancy
Miniaturization and Coloration
The Pig Who Thought He Was a Dog
Strange Hybrids
What Are We Up To?
Man and the Animal Kingdom
Animal Reaction
The Learning Process
The Syndicated Pig
How Silly Can You Get?

BIZARRE ANIMALS

Stranger than Fiction

Some existing animals are in human eyes quite as bizarre as any fictional creatures, especially in the ruses they have developed to defend themselves against enemies or the vagaries of the climate. We have innumerable examples of camouflage seen in butterflies, lizards, foxes, bears and the more uncommon chameleons and stick insects.

Others go in for more direct action. The bombardier ground-beetle when attacked by ants or picked up, ejects from its rear a kind of hot acid that can cause an uncomfortable burn. The scalding liquid is composed of chemical substances secreted in two glands, and when the insect is threatened these glands automatically discharge into a reservoir. An immediate chemical reaction takes place inside the beetle's body, heating the charge as high as the boiling point of water, then liberating free oxygen which causes it to be squirted out in a powerful jet. The beetle can shoot out upwards of 25 jets before the supply runs out. How its body resists being damaged by the intense heat is still unknown.

The larva of the Cassida or tortoise beetle uses its upturned forked tail to carry over its body a black, repulsive bag of its own excrement. Its chief enemy is the ant which at first approaches it, then strokes it with its forelegs to test its quality before it takes a bite. As soon as it does, the larva swings the bag of filthy excrement with its tail full at the ant, which beats a hasty retreat to clean itself or drag its dirty mouth-parts on the ground to rid itself of the offensive matter.

It is amazing what smaller creatures, especially insects, can produce out of their own bodies. The silkworm, which is the larva of the mulberry-eating moth spins its own cocoon, ejecting from its glands a continuous thread of some 800 to 1,200 yards in length, the raw material for our silk scarves and gowns. The spider also weaves its own silken home which it uses as a means of trapping flies and even the spider web is capable of being spun and woven into silk. In January, 1876, a Chinese delegation visited Britain and the ambassador presented to Queen Victoria an elegant silken gown which had entirely been made from thousands of spiders' webs.

Most members of the animal kingdom are, like man, possessed of five senses, but to these the shark adds a sixth. Andrianus Kalmija of the Woods Hole (Massachusetts) oceanographic institution says that sharks are guided to their prey through being able to detect weak electric fields generated unintentionally by animals in water. In addition, he believes that they use this sense to guide themselves about the ocean much as mankind uses an electromagnetic compass.

Sharks have been cruising the oceans a very long time, since before the age of the dinosaurs, and have developed over the centuries in the pores of the skin on their snouts several hundred sensory organs that can pick up the smallest differences in voltage. They can respond to a variation as minute as that which would be produced by a flashlight battery connected to electrodes *spaced a thousand miles apart in the ocean!* Little wonder that this sensitivity is believed to be the highest known in the whole of the animal kingdom.

Virgin Birth

We may pick up on very hot days lizards which seem completely dehydrated and look for all the world like bits of old leather. Yet when put into water they gradually recover and in time scuttle off as merrily as ever. An American company once marketed a product called "FISH IN A FLASH." They sold chunks of dry mud. When these were put in water tiny embryo fish which had been in a state of suspended animation for up to 3 to 4 *years* would come to life.

Stranger even than this is the whiptail lizard which has gradually spread from Mexico over the deserts of the southern United States. It is a yard long, most of its length consisting of its strong, whip-like tail with which it defends itself, and is believed to kill snakes which it uses for food.

The strangest thing about this lizard is that there are never any males. The females give birth to females without the need for male fertilization; they produce spontaneously more females and so on *ad infinitum*, every daughter looking exactly like the mother! This production of one sex only, called *parthenogenesis* is, apart from this lizard, not known in any species larger in size than the aphid or greenfly.

There have, however, been a few freak cases. In 1960, it was reported that living embryos had been developed from unfertilized hens' eggs, but that the chicks could not be studied as they had died within a few days of being hatched. In 1973, Dr. Patricia Sarvella of the United States Department of Agriculture brought to maturity four dark Cornish male chicks hatched from eggs laid by virgin hens.

Since these four were the only ones hatched out of 8,632 eggs which lived, parthenogenesis in the domestic fowl must really be freakish. Three other eggs hatched out, but all three chicks died within a week. Of the four adult males, one was mated successfully with a white Leghorn female which produced fertile eggs. The three others could not be mated.

We now know that virgin birth at least among some animals is very remotely possible, but nobody knows why or how it happens.

The Extra Senses of Animals

We know of animals in which certain senses are far more developed than they are in human beings. A dog will respond to a whistle which we ourselves cannot hear. It is impossible for us to imagine the rich sensual life of the dog, for he must live in a world in which the scent of grass, heather, hot stone, flesh, cooking, feathers and a thousand other things must transport him into spheres of ecstasy we cannot know. He will recognize a human being better by sniffing round his trouser leg than by looking him in the face. How rich his world of scents must be!

What human eye can match that of the eagle which can spot its prey from high up and swoop down with unerring accuracy? No airman can ever know the surge of primitive excitement at seeing the minute prey—and all that it means—far away below him.

For some creatures, even water has a scent. The red flying frog (Rhacephorus) or tree frog of Sumatra can sense it at a distance. If there is a ground puddle no more than the size of a dinner plate as much as 12 feet below the branch of a tree, the female frog can locate it even though it be pitch-dark. Her object in doing so is not to drink, but to breed. In the confusion of creepers and leafy branches of the tropical forest she can, by some strange means when ready to lay her eggs, climb onto that branch and find a place on it directly over the pool. She leaves her eggs on that exact spot. In time they hatch out and the young tadpoles, which cannot live unless they have water, roll off the branch and fall plop into the puddle. There they remain until, sufficiently grown, they are ready to take to the dry land and the trees.

The Friendly Dolphin

What is the mysterious link between man and dolphin? A dog, long considered man's most faithful companion and servant, has been known to turn on him, but never a dolphin.

Old sailors tell us that when the dolphins are in the vicinity there need be no fear of sharks, for the dolphin swims faster and has the advantage of any shark, whose jaw is hidden underneath its muzzle. Dolphins will attack sharks in Indian file, going for the unprotected belly, and those sharks which are not speedily put to flight will be torn open and disembowelled.

Dolphins seem to surpass most of the animal kingdom in intelligence. They have been known to take the initiative in saving deep-sea divers in distress by bringing extra oxygen capsules to them or guiding them through the depths to the surface. At the Point Mugu Naval Center in California, there is a dolphin named Tuffy who works with the divers, knows what to do in any given situation, carries out delicate missions with a minimum of instruction, all this with no sign or hint of servility, its conduct resembling rather that of a colleague than a servant.

Two things stand as barriers between the dolphin and our own kind: first, his native element is water while ours is dry land; second, while we can communicate freely in language with each other and the dolphin with his kind in his own form of speech, knowledge of each other's methods of communication is so far not much more than rudimentary.

It will probably not always be this way. The dolphin's language consists of barks, clicks and whistles in a sort of code in which, it is believed, they can talk to each other on a much higher level than any other animals.

This implies more than a little intelligence of some kind. In October, 1967, a Soviet newspaper reported that a trawler sailing in the Black Sea was suddenly accosted by a large number of dolphins, whistling loudly and indicating by their movements that something was amiss. From these it was gathered that they wanted the trawler to sail towards a particular buoy.

The nearer they approached, the more the surface of the sea was disturbed, and when they reached the buoy they found that a baby dolphin had become entangled in the meshes of a floating net. They released it amid a tumult of joyous cries and whistles from the delighted friends and relatives, who afterwards followed the trawler for miles in a sort of parade of gratitude.

Just as humans are slowly piercing the communication veil, individual dolphins are learning human language. One has been made to understand and speak some twenty words of English—not much but a beginning. Incredible as it may seem, two dolphins in Seattle, Washington, had a telephone chat in their own language which lasted the best part of a half-hour.

"When scientists have succeeded in deciphering the language of the dolphins," says a Russian professor, "they are very likely to discover some hitherto unpublished information about man's past." He believes that both go back to the second tertiary period at the same time as tapirs, parrots and Barbary ducks appeared, and that, between the two—dolphin and man—there has been a close sentimental affinity ever since.

If we ever manage to fathom the dolphin's mode of speech we may also find that there is between them a well-developed kind of language, rudimentary in human beings, *a language not based on reason.*

It may follow that, in the development of reason to the detriment of other now mysterious animal functions, human beings took a retrograde step away from some Golden Age towards a civilization dominated by every kind of envy, ambition and all the other deadly sins to which we are heirs.

It's worth thinking about. Put that calculator away for a while.

Animals Outperform Humans

When the ordinary human flea takes off on a leap he goes from standstill to 100 centimetres a second in less than two thousandths of a second, subjecting himself to a force of 150G or 150 times the force of gravity, roughly the same as driving a car into a brick wall at 200 miles per hour. A bee can haul a burden more than 300 times its own weight. To accomplish anything parallel to this a sixteen-stone (224-lb) man would have to drag along a 30-ton vehicle.

The leech is a parasite normally living in water, and it has developed suckers to attach itself to another living body and suck its blood. In jungles and swamps the many varieties of leeches are a peril to human life, but they have their uses elsewhere. In olden times a doctor would put anything from eight to twelve leeches on a patient if he needed blood-letting, and even today they are often used. A number were once shown on a British television programme and when it was over, nobody knowing quite what to do with them, left them to the cleaner who tipped them down the lavatory. Next morning the first person to use the lavatory was the attendant. Within minutes he had to be rushed to hospital for treatment.

The common barnacle starts life as a free-swimming active embryo which, when it attains adulthood, attaches itself to the bottoms of ships, to pylons, posts, driftwood or whatever objects may be near. There it remains, as Professor Julian Huxley once said, "fixed by its head and kicking its food into its mouth with its legs." To do this it produces a glue in its body twice as strong as epoxy, binding together any materials and resisting all chemicals known to science. It can be chilled to minus 383°F and still does not crack. A mere 3/10,000ths of an inch of barnacle glue provides a strength of more than three tons. The glue comes from glands which appear in the final larval stage of its life when it is ready to attach itself to its permanent home. At this point it approaches the object chosen, strikes it head first and from the glands the glue is poured, fixing it permanently.

The number of animal characteristics which seem bizarre to man is infinite, and with the increase in knowledge of the natural world they get more and more as time passes. We know that many animals which eat only vegetation get enough liquid in their diet and have no need to drink; among these are the gazelle and the gorilla. Shark steaks, which are eaten in various parts of the world, have no fat on them because the shark secretes all the fat it needs in its liver. Moreover the white shark never gets sick and is immune to cancer.

We all know about flying fish, but who has heard of the hiccoughing fish? Yet there is one in South American waters that gulps air and then belches so loudly that it can be heard for miles.

The Sea Horse, a Pregnant Male

Anybody who has visited the shores of the Mediterranean will have seen the beautiful minute *Hippocampus* or sea horse which is often caught, dried and sold to tourists as an ornament or trinket. It is strange that the sea horse, usually no more than about three inches in length, ever manages to survive with so many marine predators around. It is a poor swimmer, swimming, as it were, standing up and going from place to place with the aid of a single dorsal fin. This, placed in the middle of the body and going from side to side about 70 times a second, moves it slowly along. It can take as long as five minutes to travel about three feet. It cannot resist being carried away by currents and has to remain in or about the same place by curling its tail around seaweed or coral where it finds enough food and shelter. Its coloration, blending with the background, gives it protection from enemies.

One of the strangest things about the sea horse is that the male gives birth. The female produces the eggs, then deposits them in a pouch at the base of the male's tail. From that time on, father becomes "pregnant" and after an incubation of 10 to 45 days depending on the species, the little sea horses appear with what seem to be rhythmic "labour pains" as father's pouch opens and closes repeatedly, releasing the small fry in groups of 50 or more at a time. Depending on the species, as many as 700 of the tiny creatures can come from the same hatching, but at least 90 out of every hundred are greedily snapped up as soon as they appear, in the jaws of other hungry creatures.

The Thorny Hedgehog

Defence systems are very interesting. One we know best is that of the common hedgehog which, on the first hint of danger, even an unusual sound, can cause a large muscle on the underside of its body to contract suddenly and let the hedgehog roll itself into a round ball covered with hundreds of small sharp spines.

This, however, is not all, for the hedgehog has a second line of defence. Its main diet is insects, but it does not turn away from other small creatures such as mice, lizards, frogs and toads. The toad is specially important to it, for, behind its eyes are the parotid or salivary glands which in the case of the toad are incorporated in the skin tissue. The secretion they contain is a poisonous substance, and the hedgehog, when it catches a toad, first bites and chews this part, mixing its secretions with its own saliva until a sort of froth is produced. With this froth the hedgehog coats his spines. Any creature coming into contact with them gets an extremely unpleasant injection of the poison.

The hedgehog is adept at making this frothy substance and if the toad is not at hand, will use any sort of irritant it can get—tobacco, sour milk, soap or even the juice of plants to mix with its saliva.

This frothy anointing of the spines is an ingrained habit, for the young, even before they open their eyes for the first time, may be seen creating the froth and licking it onto their spines.

The Lemming's Death March

One of the strangest of the small animals is the lemming, a member of the mouse tribe and itself not much larger than the domestic mouse. Its principal habitat is the high lands or fells of the great central mountain chain of Scandinavia, plateaus above the fir-clad slopes covered mainly with dwarf birch and juniper. There under tussocks of grass or dry straws the lemming constructs its hair-lined nest in which the female would normally produce two breeds of three to eight young in a season. This, compared with some animals, is not a high birth rate. But in a cold climate such as Scandinavia, the breeding grounds of the lemming at certain intervals (varying between 5 and 20 years) become overpopulated.

It is then that the lemming population of a whole region starts its long trek to the sea and eventual mass suicide. What decides the moment for this strange mass movement to commence is still a mystery, but at this moment, impelled by some instinct to make for lower and lusher feeding grounds, they migrate, the whole body moving forward slowly, always in the same direction down the valleys, eating everything in their way, all the time growing in numbers by breeding more rapidly than they did in their natural homes.

The migration may last for from two to three years during which all the land over which they pass is devastated and crops consumed, bringing ruin as surely as if a plague of locusts had passed over it. This is not only due to the lemmings, but also to the many beasts and birds of prey—bears, wolves, foxes, wild cats, stoats, weasels, eagles, hawks and owls which attack them. Farmers, anxious to get the lemmings off their land, pursue them with dogs, while they are trampled into the ground by horses, cattle, goats and reindeer.

Yet nothing can stop their progress. They travel by night always in the same direction, sometimes staying in one place for longer periods, then off again, swimming streams, rivers and even lakes several miles wide until they come to the greatest "lake" of all, the sea. They can hardly know that here is a stretch of water they will never cross, and they enter it as one, swimming out and farther out. Every single one perishes.

Recently two American researchers have discovered new and strange facts about these curious little animals. They have within them substances which not only save life under normal conditions, but can destroy it under abnormal ones. In the depth of winter when other animals, some large, some small, hibernate, subjecting their bodies to a sort of suspended animation, the lemming remains awake and active because its body, by some strange chemical action, creates its own anti-freeze which keeps the blood flowing throughout the severe weather. In a normal Scandinavian winter this maintains life until spring, when the thaw gradually comes. There are, however, sometimes freak periods when in winter the tundra is affected by a sudden warm spell. Near Point Barrow in Alaska where the habits of the little animal were being studied, it was found that the sudden thaw upset the lemming's internal anatomy so that the blood, proof against frost, coagulated in the winter thaw, giving it thrombosis and killing it.

What this anti-freeze is nobody yet knows, but there are hopes that the formula will one day be found and that it may be of use when planes come down in the Arctic and passengers are subjected to severe weather conditions. Some researchers believe that it may be this anti-freeze which sparks off the lemming migrations, arguing that overpopulation in the homelands produces a hormone which releases it, and that the change in blood composition within their bodies drives them wild so that they run madly on and on, following the line of least resistance until they either drop dead from exhaustion or plunge to their deaths in the sea.

Powers of Endurance

In the summer of 1977, Van Price, a rancher, took his dog Keeno, a two-year-old Australian dingo bitch, into the Idaho desert on a round-up of stray cattle. Somehow she became separated from her owner and, try as he might to track her, he could find no lead. He was convinced she wouldn't survive. "There's nothing there but rattlesnakes, lava and coyotes," he said. "The only water is the Lost River."

As time passed Price began receiving phone calls. Here and there the bitch had been seen. Ranchers had hailed her as she crossed their land, but she would stop for nobody. She ran on, and her master eventually gave her up for lost.

Four months later she appeared in Butte City, Idaho, about 20 miles from Price's ranch in Darlington. Somehow she had made a journey of 50 miles in the hottest part of the summer through a desert with no food supply worth mentioning, and no water. What is more, she was found to be dragging a coyote trap which had caught her by the foot. Nobody could catch her, and it was only after a group of children had made friends with her that a grown-up could get close enough to her to take off the trap. The leg was crushed.

Nobody knows how the dog could have survived. But everybody agreed that it was more than a miracle that she had survived at all. Now she is home and happy minus the leg, which had to be amputated.

A similar feat of endurance was that of a sheep in Bogart, Scotland, which, during the hard winter of 1977–8, was buried for 25 days deep in a snowdrift, then discovered by a sheepdog and dug out. It too recovered.

The World of the Grasshopper

Nature cannot produce a winner every time. It certainly can't in the case of the grasshopper whose strange goings-on have been investigated by Robert Willey, a biologist at the University of Illinois Circle Campus. He observes them in the Colorado Rockies, often tracking individuals by painting spots on their backs to follow their activities through binoculars.

But there are difficulties. If the spots are too bright his subjects become the menus for birds' dinners; if too dull, he is in danger of losing sight of them altogether!

The arphia grasshopper, a winged variety living in the Rockies, has its own unique defence against the cold. Over the winter it may freeze solid, becoming crystallized all through its body, but the glycerin in its cells allows it to survive the cold and to resume normal activity when it attains full maturity with the coming of spring.

"Trying to think like a grasshopper is very important," says Willey, though he admits that at times it is difficult because the insect becomes thoroughly confused. In fable it has been celebrated as an example of improvidence, heedlessness and foolhardiness. When we learn from Willey that he has seen males trying to mate with sticks, thermometers and the edges of cardboard cartons we can understand why.

Freaks of Nature

Investigating teams have recently been studying the strange activities of certain seagulls on Santa Barbara Island off the California coast just north of Los Angeles. Here, because of the scarcity of male birds, some of the females have taken to moving in with each other.

Dr. George Hunt of the University of California who received a grant for this purpose studied the conduct of some 1,200 pairs and reported that when this happened one of the females adopted a male role, the birds forming stable unions like those of heterosexual seagulls, going through the motions of mating, laying sterile eggs and defending their nests just like other couples did.

"We were absolutely astounded," wrote Dr. Hunt. "This sort of thing has not been found before and was clearly not what we anticipated."

It is in the true freaks that we find the truly bizarre, but in the animal kingdom they are rare indeed—a gosling with four legs born in Kazan, Central Russia, in 1977; a cat with four ears, the property of a steelworker, born in 1976, two of the ears being undeveloped with no hearing apparatus; a sheepdog in East Germany which grew two sets of ears in 1973; and a kitten born in 1977 with 24 claws, seven on each front paw and five on each back paw. But these are no more than nine-day wonders and are quickly forgotten.

Then there are animals which, it is claimed, have given birth to very unlikely crossbreeds. In Dawlish Ford, Somerset, England, in May, 1971, a swan paired with a gander and laid six eggs. Villagers fondly hoped for the hatching of a brood of "sweese" but no record exists of that ever happening. In Knaresborough, Yorkshire, in 1974 a rabbit reportedly took a fancy to Gertie, a guinea pig, and thirty days later "bunny pig" arrived having a guinea pig's body and a rabbit's ears. "Frankly, it's a bit of an embarrassment," said the owner of the zoo. To the parents or the zoo?

The word *mule* is often applied to the result of matings such as these and is synonymous with "hybrid." It is applied to birds bred in this way by canary fanciers, but mainly to the offspring of horse and ass, the true mule being the hybrid of a male jackass with a mare, and the less valuable *hinny,* the offspring of a stallion and a female ass.

And here is where human agency comes into the picture.

Breeding for Use and Fancy

Ever since the first domestic animals were brought into his home by man, he has carried out experiments in breeding. His earliest experience was probably with the dog, which may have been evolved from a wolf, a jackal, coyote, or from some early and now extinct canine species. However that may be, there is no domestic animal which has undergone through selective breeding such an extraordinary amount of variation in size, proportion of limbs, ears and tail. As the poet W. M. Letts wrote:

"It's wonderful dogs they're breeding now:
Small as a flea and large as a cow."

Inevitably freaks are produced, not by the legitimate breeding for use within a species, but by the selection and mating of animals within that species to over-emphasize one particular feature.

In a recent contest in West Berlin, a hare was put into the arena and won the prize for an ear length of 26 inches, the record for the lop-eared English Ram breed being 27. "A vulgar display of excess," snapped one bitter spectator.

In the domestication of animals, there comes a stage in which, when breeding is carried out simply to exaggerate a single feature, such as the ears, the snub or long nose, the hair or the short legs, the life of the animal produced can become a misery or even its very survival may be prejudiced. How long, for instance, would a hare, dragging ears more than a foot long across open country, be able to survive unaided?

Miniaturization and Coloration

In these days man can do almost anything the law allows with animals. A method of stunting their growth has been developed by a professor of a Spanish university which involves the removal of the thyroid gland. One side-effect is that the animal also loses all aggressive instincts, becomes completely docile and "a perfect companion."

The genetic engineers at Cambridge predict that if you had the money and inclination, you could possess a rhino called Rover and take him on a walk in the park at the end of a dog lead.

To prove his point the professor produced a "micro" horse which, even though fully grown, could be picked up and cuddled.

While most people are revolted by this kind of deliberate operation, such undersized animals are, of course, occasionally born in nature. Dwarfs also appear in humankind, and this does not always imply deformity. John Jarvis, page to Mary I, Queen of England, was less than 3 feet high and Jeffery Hudson, who served Charles I, was not any taller, but he took part in the Civil War and was captured, first by the Dunkirkers and later by the Turks. The most famous dwarf of all was Charles Stratton known as General Tom Thumb, billed as 30½ inches tall, who was exhibited all over the world. One of his most famous exploits was to fight a duel with a turkey. His weapon was a knitting needle! The contest started after Tom was "served" to the King inside a pie crust.

The name Tom Thumb was also given to a horse only 28 inches high which was popular at agricultural shows all over Britain. A circus offered his owner Mr. Graham Aston £3,000 for him, then one night in 1976 he was stolen from a field at Henley-in-Arden where he was spending the winter. He was probably smuggled abroad and nothing more appears to have been heard of him.

A somewhat different story, not of miniaturization but of coloration comes from Hertfordshire, England, where Mr. Ernest Ebbitson, a museum caretaker, has taken 30 years to evolve an orange-hued frog, selecting for his work ordinary common frogs of the lightest shade he could find.

"I wanted an orange frog because you can see right through them. It's like looking at an X-ray. I am hoping that my work will end the wanton dissection of frogs at universities where thousands are used each year."

Mr. Ebbitson hopes to keep up the breeding of the new strain in his well-protected "froggery" until their numbers are large enough to allow for their dispatch to universities for study and research.

The Pig Who Thought He Was a Dog

There is a well established process in animals called imprinting. If the natural parents are removed from a newborn animal or bird, the baby will often adopt the first creature it sees as its parent to copy.

While writing this I am reminded of Leslie, who flourished in our back yard during the hungry years of World War I. Leslie was the smallest piglet in one of several litters we raised as part of the war food effort, and though the other seven within six months were growing apace, Leslie hardly added more than a few inches to his stature. That may be why he became a family pet. He made friends with the dog, played and walked out with it and must really have thought he was himself a dog. He would go with us along the village street to fetch the groceries to the amused glances and remarks of everyone, and he would wait outside the shop door, then follow us back home again, all the while giving contented little squeals. He never developed a full adult pig's grunt.

Everybody around knew Leslie and he feared nobody. They say that pigs are highly intelligent animals; perhaps that is why George Orwell made the dictator Napoleon of *Animal Farm* a pig. But Leslie was no Napoleon; he was amiable and tractable. The only thing he didn't like was being picked up.

In 1977 a chicken at an animal sanctuary in Worcestershire, England, was seen to behave in much the same way as Leslie. She ate beef and biscuits at the dog's feeding bowl, slept in a basket inside a cupboard and was known to have chased a fox. "It's incredible," said the sanctuary owner. "The only thing she can't do is bark."

There was in 1978 a similar case in Sebring, Florida. A young Brahmin bull called Easter jumps up and down bellowing when the cows are rounded up, and gobbles up the dog food even before the dog can get at it. "In fact," says its owner, "he thinks he's a dog, but what will happen when he grows to full size nobody knows. I expect we shall have to pen him up."

I can believe stories like this. After all, I knew Leslie.

Strange Hybrids

It has long been known that interbreeding between members of the same tribe of animals is possible. It was in ancient times that the people of Asia Minor first crossed the horse with the ass and produced that most hardy and useful animal, the mule.

Such interbreeding has become more common during recent times, not primarily to produce useful animals but partly to inform the scientist about whether the more distantly related species of the same family or even species of different families will mate and produce young.

Take, for instance, the donkey and the zebra, both members of the horse genus. One is striped, the other not, one is wild and the other a domestic animal, so that we might unjustifiably consider them more distantly related than the horse and the donkey. Yet in Colchester, England, in 1971 a male zebra and a female donkey were mated and produced a hybrid to which they gave the name Zedonk. In this quite attractive hybrid the zebra's stripes were seen only on the legs.

The British Commonwealth Bureau of Animal Breeding and Genetics has prepared stocklists of such mammalian hybrids comprising about 500, while the companion volume on birds has several times as many entries.

Members of the cat family have also been crossed with each other, the *liger*, having a lion as father, and the *tigon*, having a tiger as father. Perhaps the most bizarre of all time was the offspring of a male lion and a hybrid between a puma and a leopard. It was thus half lion, one quarter puma and one quarter leopard. The problem was to name such a creature—the lipumard?

The hybrid of the bear family, a cross between a polar bear and a brown bear changed from white to brown and back to white again as it grew up.

Different species of cattle have not been too difficult to mate, and have sometimes produced useful variations. The sheep family *(Ovis)* and goats *(Capra)* belong to the horned ruminants or *Bovidae* as, of course, do cattle. The domestic sheep and goat mate readily enough and conception occurs. But the embryo has up to recently always been aborted before birth. The Russians have apparently overcome this rejection problem. Through the use of drugs similar to those used in transplant operations, they have produced a live sheep-goat hybrid. A reliable report has recently come in from East Germany that in 1977 a pet goat gave birth to an animal seeming to be half goat and half sheep—the first known to have been bred without human interference. A *shoat* or a *geep?*

Dogs, as one would imagine, interbreed readily with wolves and jackals. The dog and the fox were both included by the great Swedish botanist Linnaeus in the same genus *(Canis)*, but are today regarded as separate. It has never been possible to produce a hybrid between the two.

It is in the field of genetic engineering proper, however, that the developments really rival Frankenstein.

In Brookhaven Institute in America and in Cambridge University, England, scientists are now successfully producing a totally new form of life. They have fused together animal and vegetable cells to produce an organism part animal, part vegetable. What is more the animal cells were those of a human female.

Although this sounds like the worst fears of science fiction writers come true, the objective of the experiment is actually very praiseworthy. The ultimate aim is to produce a plant that tastes like and has the nutrition of meat. If fully successful it would go a long way to solving the world's food problem, as we could "grow" meat directly like we grow wheat—without "converting" it inefficiently through killing a sheep or a cow.

What Are We Up To?

One question arises. How far are we to go with this kind of experimentation? Scientifically it may be valid, for the experimenter may tell us that anything which increases the volume of human knowledge is permissible.

The question is: Are there limits? Now we know that, as a general rule, the nearer related one species of a family is to another, the more likely it is that a hybrid can be produced *but* that the hybrid is probably going to be infertile. The point is, if that hybrid is not of use to the human race, as the mule is, or likely to be of use except as a specimen or perhaps a public spectacle, is there any justification for repeating the experiment and producing more of the same kind?

More serious still, where does the human being come into this?

We, with the apes, monkeys, lemurs etc. are part of the world's living creatures and are classified among them under the name of primates. Hence the comment, in passing, which appeared in a newspaper in the early seventies:

"There are no known cases of human hybrids of any kind."

An ominous comment? We add in full, a report in a daily newspaper of August, 1976.

DON'T MAKE A MONSTER

The most horrifying news this week comes from the staid International Primate Society Conference in Cambridge.

We humans are primates. So are monkeys. And it seems that the biologists are within a needle's plunge of making an even closer connection between us and the apes. By mating humans with chimps.

American scientists reckon they can crossbreed men and monkeys. The biologist working on the technique describes it as *incredibly intriguing from a scientific point of view.*

Incredibly intriguing it may be. But useful, kind and human it is not. The offspring wouldn't be human. It would be a monkey.

But it would probably be able to think about its own tragedy.

The scientist Dr. Geoffrey Bourne says: 'I wonder whether I have the right to bring a creature into the world that would be neither fish, nor fowl.'

Dr. Bourne, you haven't!

Man and the Animal Kingdom

It is generally agreed that man has evolved from some species of the family of primates which has now disappeared from the face of the earth. He lives, but his grandfather is long since dead. Nevertheless he has several more or less distant relatives living among the trees in forests dotted about the globe. But these are very different from him—so different that he has been able through his superior abilities to control their growth, to rob them of their forest homes, even to take them prisoner and confine them in his zoos and safari parks.

The difference between him and them is that somehow he, probably through the struggle for existence over the ages, has been given the upright stance, a hand with a reversible thumb (very important this), a larynx that can produce a wide range of pitch, a mouth that can convert the sound into intelligible language and, to govern and direct all these faculties, an intelligence housed in a brain that can reason and think in abstract terms.

"Think like a grasshopper," said the American expert. Is it remotely possible that any one of us can even think like a dog, a cat or a horse, or can have even the remotest idea of what the world is like to any one of these creatures?

One thing is clear. The dog knows man, his master. But if his master accustoms him to associate the word *man* with an enemy, he will go for that enemy whatever it may be. In other words, he can't think of the general *man* and apply the term to all men, *stick* to all sticks, *lamp-post* to all lamp-posts, *dinner* to all dinners and so on. Much less can he think of abstracts such as light, dark, hot or cold. So, not having a grasp of concepts, which these are, he is unable to handle them or to reason. If he could do this he would be man's equal, capable of speculation and invention, which he is not.

We hear so many people say of their pets, "He understands every word I say." But he doesn't, for he hasn't the mental equipment to do so. In fact, humanity is so far in advance of the rest of the animal kingdom in this sort of mental activity that a certain number of people believe that the origin of mankind was not on this earth at all, but in some other part of the universe from which our most distant forefathers migrated. Here when they landed they may have found other beings and interbred with them to produce mankind. We need not necessarily go that far. For our purpose it doesn't matter very much.

Animal Reaction

Members of the animal kingdom do not think as we do, they react. In Norway, ravens have taken to attacking hang-gliders, seeing in them some strange and possibly menacing member of their own kind. They not only divebomb them but also appear to be about to slash at the fabric with their beaks and claws. So far they have not torn the fabric of any glider, but if they do it could lose its buoyancy and go out of control.

The same kind of thing happened in Italy in 1978, this time the assailant being an eagle. Antonio Beozzi was soaring 4,600 feet above the mountains north of Turin when an eagle suddenly dived on him, attacked the windshield and broke into the cockpit. "I was very scared," he said. "It snapped at my arms. We had a tough fight until I grabbed its neck and strangled it." Holding onto the dead eagle with his left hand Beozzi brought the single-person glider back to earth.

Beozzi's eagle mistook the glider for some strange bird. According to legend another eagle in ancient Greece made a mistake which had more serious consequences. The playwright Aeschylus was bald and the eagle, mistaking his shining pate for a rock, dropped a tortoise on his head and killed him. A natural reaction on the part of a hungry bird of prey.

No less natural was the reaction of the camel which had broken out of a circus and was walking along a street in Hamburg one day in 1977. A motorist driving along the street became confused and accidentally struck the camel's leg. The impact was not serious, but the infuriated animal turned, drummed on the front of the car with its front hooves and smashed the windscreen. The driver lost control and rammed a parked car.

A costly disaster befell Mr. Bejoy Khar, a Pakistani living in Birmingham, England. He had laboriously saved £30 ($60) to buy a new suit and was wearing it one day for the first time. Unfortunately for him he took his walk along the bank of a river and had not gone far when he saw a dog struggling for its life in the water. Mr. Khar gallantly jumped in to save it. The dog, unmindful of the fact that Mr. Khar was trying to save its life, gave him a nasty bite as he grabbed it. Worse, his brand new suit had to be sent to the cleaner.

Mr. Khar mused after his heroics—"The funny thing is, I don't really like dogs."

An animal when threatened acts in one of two ways—either it attacks or it tries to run away. Often before an attack it gives ominous signs; a dog does this by baring its teeth. The gorilla, on the other hand, though fearsome to look at, is a gentle animal. If he feels threatened he puts out his tongue, often following this with a sudden leap forward, but rarely attacking.

The strangest encounters between animals have been known to occur. In the city streets on Chicago's North Side, according to an officer of the Animal Care and Control Office, witnesses had seen stray chickens attack and rout a number of inquisitive dogs. They spread their wings, put their heads close to the ground and charged. The dogs, never having seen chickens take up this pose before, ran away, their tails between their legs.

Many an animal generally considered savage will turn tail for no apparent reason. The jaguar, one of the most dangerous of the big cats, is said to be afraid of all dogs, no matter what size they are.

Instinctive reaction to human beings is often, as in the case of Mr. Khar, sudden and unexpected. Mr. Buthar Singh was an Indian travel agent who was one day shaving himself, using the surface of Lake Rannan, North Borneo, as a mirror. Suddenly a fresh-water turtle, possibly mistaking his nose for a tasty morsel, rose from the depths, seized it and dragged Mr. Singh under the surface. "It was an act of God," said the unlucky travel agent. "My father warned me never to shave myself, but I had to do it to please the tourists."

Sometimes the animal's reaction is simple enough. An Australian jockey, Keith Smith, out for a day's fishing, was not so lucky. He was surprised when he hooked a large and very lively fish. All his efforts to land it were in vain, but he held on to his rod. During the struggle, instead of the man catching the fish the fish caught the man. It pulled him into the Murray River where he was drowned.

Agatha Christie's Irish chauffeur, however, was quite casual about the demise of his uncle. He told her that he had been present when his Uncle Fred had been eaten by a crocodile in Burma. "I didn't know what to do about it really. However, we thought the best thing was to have the crocodile stuffed, so we did, and got it sent home to his wife." History does not recall her reaction.

Food, of course, exerts an irresistible attraction to animals. The seven bears in Chicago's zoo which were separated from the snack bar by no more than a moat, had for a long time shown great interest in what was going on across the water. One night there was a heavy downpour and next morning when the keeper arrived he found that the moat had been flooded, all the bears had swum across it and were in the bar, smothered with the remains of a gigantic meal consisting of ice cream and marshmallows.

The Learning Process

Many of the higher animals can be taught to perform actions, some quite complicated. Del-Rita, a seven-year-old elephant in Puck's Canadian Circus has been taught to swim, and takes her daily dip in Lake Ontario. In underwater swimming she has the advantage over man as her trunk acts as a snorkel.

Parrots, without knowing what they are saying, can repeat word for word and tone for tone the sounds taught them, and their replies are sometimes coincidentally very apt. A coach-load of tourists once converged on a Yorkshire inn crowding the bar and asking for drinks. The licensee kept a parrot which, especially when there was a little excitement, tended to get in his way, as it did on this occasion when he was drawing the pints. "Look out, Polly," he said.

The reply, to the amazement of the customers, came pat: "What the 'ell have I done?"

Parrots can sometimes cause more acute embarrassment. In Douglas, Isle of Man, the conductors of the horse-drawn trams were puzzled when the horses, which usually stopped at the conductor's whistle, started to draw up at a point between two halts. Soon, no journey was ever made without this happening. It was eventually found that in one of the nearby houses there was a parrot which had learned to reproduce perfectly the conductor's whistle. After it had been moved to a room where the horses could no longer hear it, the nuisance stopped.

Monkeys, of course, are good mimics and a monkey recently succeeded in thumbing a lift from Nice to Cannes—a distance of 24 miles. And when some of the citizens of West Covina, California, brought a case against a certain Mr. Davis alleging that his pet chimpanzee, Moe, was dangerous, the judge in court disagreed. "From what I've seen," he said, "Moe is better behaved than a lot of humans that get brought in here."

When acquitted, Moe, who was dressed in a checked shirt, yellow whipcord trousers and two-tone bootees, jumped on the bench and shook Judge Crumb by the hand.

From feats such as these performed by animals it would appear that they do possess the power to reason, but this is not so. Two more accounts may help us to understand how their learning is on a different level.

In Denver, Colorado, mules were used to draw tracked trolley cars up the hills and, as an incentive they were put on the rear platform of the cars for the downhill run. This they evidently enjoyed for, when some of the mules were disposed of, one was bought by a farmer. He put it to work with the plough, but found that whenever it reached the crest of a hilly field it tried to jump on the plough. It had laboriously to be taught another routine before it was any use.

Bill Fedeler was the owner of a grain mill in Alpha, Iowa, and he owned a 14-month-old Doberman named Hyde. Knowing the nuisance and the danger which can be caused by dogs barking in cars, he had taught the puppy never to make a sound when in the car. On December 3rd, 1977, when he looked for her, she was missing.

"She wouldn't run away on her own," said Fedeler. "I figured someone had stolen her."

Christmas came and went and Hyde did not return. It was January 4th, more than a month after her disappearance that an acquaintance of Fedeler took a potential buyer to see an old

Ford car that was kept behind the mill.

When they looked inside there was the dog, reduced almost to a skeleton, but alive. Somebody had evidently lured her into the old car and shut her in. There she had remained without food in temperatures as low as 17 below zero in a car within a few yards of every passerby and on a pathway along which one woman passed every morning to empty a bin. All that time the dog had not made a sound.

Again, re-education had to begin.

The Syndicated Pig

How do you syndicate a pig?

Mark Cowley of Waterhole, northern Nevada, population about 50, has an alcoholic pig born May 1st, 1974, and named Waterhole Ike. Every morning the pig comes into Cowley's cafe tavern and drinks his fill of beer from a five-gallon bucket.

The idea of syndicating the pig came in 1976 when the beer-drinking pig began to get locally famous. Cowley thought that since you can syndicate a racehorse to the tune of a few millions one ought to be able to do the same for a pig to the tune of a few hundreds. So he and eight of his patrons formed the syndicate and put the money into a cigar-box. In time the funds outgrew the capacity of the cigar-box to accommodate them and a savings account had to be opened. But the bank they approached said that a social security number was needed for the holder so that the interest could be reported to the Internal Revenue Service.

So Cowley applied for a Social Security card for the pig, putting down the mother's name as Go-Pig-Go and the father's as Three Stars, which was true. Not quite knowing what to sign at the foot of the form, since no pig can write its name, he put "Waterhole Ike by Mark Cowley." Soon the Department sent the card and he gave the number to the bank.

Then he went to the welfare people and told them he knew

that Waterhole Ike couldn't work because he was an alcoholic with ten dependents. The Welfare Department was on the point of giving him $650 a month when it was told the true facts. Cowley believes he might have been able to get him into the alcoholic rehabilitation plan, but had that been done his fame as an alcoholic pig would have been at an end.

Shortly afterwards the bank wrote the pig a letter stating that he was eligible to borrow $250 to $2,500 at any of their statewide branches, and the letter was solemnly read to the pig on the morning of its arrival, as all the many other fan letters are read to it.

In February, 1978, the pig had about $1,000 in the bank, enough to supply him with beer for the time being.

The point is this. Is it Waterhole Ike the alcoholic pig who is bizarre, or his promoters?

How Silly Can You Get?

Mr. Sean Wilby, answering a police charge of cruelty for biting his dog, explained that they did a trick together. When he said "Grrh, grrh!" the dog had learned to jump in the air and he caught it in his mouth. The bite, he said, was just a mistake.

Annual frog kissing and jumping contests are held in Calaveras County, California. Frog jumping is well known; frog kissing is not. "All you have to do," says one of the promoters, "is to kiss a frog and turn him into a handsome prince and you'll get a million dollars. If you can't manage to do that but are still feeling creative, the Golden Wart will be awarded for the sexiest frog kiss. Just for having the guts to kiss the frog you'll be given a horny toad."

A world champion snail race held annually in England at Folkestone was won by Festina Lente (hasten slowly), a Kentish snail who did the full distance of 28 inches in 4 minutes 50.8 seconds.

Señor Felix Perez, head of the experimental surgery department of Madrid University, has invented a set of steel dentures suitable for cows. "Once a cow is fitted with a full set," he says, "its life-span will be extended, its sex life will improve and its milk production will soar."

In the city of Charleston, South Carolina, tourists are taken around town by horse carriage. In 1975, the officials decided in the interests of street cleanliness, to equip all horses with diapers. After nine days the order was withdrawn but there was such a clamour on the part of those living in the city's historic streets that it had to be re-introduced.

A psychology teacher in Greenwich Village, New York City, also concerned about street nuisances, thinks that dogs should have their own lavatories. So he had a 36-inch-bowl sunk in the pavement outside his apartment in the middle of which was a pipe with an automatic flush valve. As an incentive to attract the dogs he used biscuits. But, this specimen being designed for males, he decided to experiment with a female version, using a scent that would attract lady pets.

Which brings us back to the original speculation, that the bizarre, like beauty, may after all be in the eye of the beholder.

BIZARRE CUSTOMS

The Toast, the Kiss and the Handshake
How Much for a Wife?
Ordeal and Bull-Roarer
The Knot
Conjugal Rights
Hospitality Gone Mad
Touched for the Evil
Woman and Child
Fashion and Fad
Vain Man!
The Last Act

BIZARRE CUSTOMS

The Toast, the Kiss and the Handshake

"Drink to me only with thine eyes,
And I will pledge with mine:
Or leave a kiss within the cup
And I'll not ask for wine."

The Romans drank each other's health in wine into which pieces of spiced, burned bread had been dropped to enhance its taste. Seventeenth century England copied the ancient custom, from which the phrase "to drink a toast" originated. Thus the word referred first to the burnt bread, then to the drink and now to the ceremony.

The French have borrowed from England and speak of *porter un toast*—to bring a toast; the Germans use their own language calling it *ein Trinksprüch* "a drink-speech"; the Italians took from Germany the very words of the toast—*bring die Sie,* "I bring (luck) to you," and they call the toast *un brindisi,* while the Spaniards take the best of both worlds using the English *tostar* and the German *brindar* "to toast." The European Common (Language) Market!

Ben Jonson would have none of it. His lady's eyes were enough to call forth his own pledge of a loving glance. But there still remains the cup in which his lady is asked to leave a kiss instead of wine. Did Ben Jonson know that, according to Greek historians, kissing began when menfolk wanted to know if their women had been sipping wine on the quiet? A kiss on the lips was enough to furnish a clue.

This is by no means the whole story as our Latin vocabulary tells us, for the kiss, only customary in Britain and America among close friends and between male and females or two females, is also more widely used as a salutation. The Romans had three words for it—*osculum* from which we have the word "osculation" and which was confined to the cheek; *basium* (French *baiser,* Spanish *besar,* Italian *baciare*), a kiss implanted on the lips, and *suavium* which was a tender kiss between lovers and we may be sure it had nothing to do with wine.

Except for the kissing of the Pope's toe the kiss of humility has disappeared. Some Europeans still kiss the hand as a greeting for both sexes, and even where this custom is no longer practiced it remains in correspondence—*Pongame Vd a los pies q.b.* (que beso) *de su señora*—"put me at the feet, which I kiss, of your lady," or in blunt English, "give my kind regards to your wife." The word *besalamano* "I kiss your hand," or BLM is used at the end of a letter in Spain without a signature.

Away with learning! The more widely used greeting is now the handshake which originated in the meeting of strangers who, both wishing to prove that their intentions were peaceful, held out the right or weapon hand as a gesture. Some doctors today warn us against the handshake on the ground that flu and other germs are passed in this way from one person to another.

A Chinese was accustomed to greet a friend by shaking his own hand, not that of his friend. A Hindu still puts his hands together, palm to palm and bows low. Perhaps if we really cared about each other's health it might be preferable to do as the Russians do when meeting a friend and give him or her a bear-hug. The French go that bit further, combining the hug with the *osculum* on each cheek and call it *embrasser* "to embrace" or, in ceremonial meetings they give a token touch cheek to cheek, right and left.

Bizarre Europeans! Others, equally bizarre, give salutations by taking off their shoes, rubbing noses, cracking fingers. Among the Masai tribesmen of Tanzania, spitting is regarded as an indication of reverence and goodwill. Newborn children are spat upon by those who wish to endow them with good luck. Masai will spit at each other when they meet and spit at each other again to say goodbye. To conclude a bargain two traders will spit at each other. In medieval Japan, when two gentlemen wished to seal an agreement, they urinated together, criss-crossing their streams of urine.

With all these disadvantages, the handshake, despite the germs seems rather more practical!

In some strange way spitting is associated with power. One sees it in certain films, especially Westerns in which the villain or some other obnoxious character follows up a good round oath with a well-aimed gobbet—a sort of assertion of virility.

Even among little boys there is, or used to be, a catching game played in the streets in which one side ran after and caught members of the other side, and, one by one imprisoned them in a "den" marked out on the ground. One might be caught, but you were not fully captive unless, while being held, you had been spit over by your captor.

How Much for a Wife?

"'I won't sell her for less than five,' said the husband bringing down his fist so that the basins danced. 'I'll sell her for five guineas to any man that will pay me the money, and treat her well; and he shall have her for ever, and never hear ought o' me. But she shan't go for less. Now then—five guineas—and she's yours.'"

This is the account of how Michael Henchard, later to be Mayor of Casterbridge, sold his wife. It's fiction, but Thomas Hardy took the idea from episodes in real life. Take the following account from the *Times* of Wednesday, December 31st, 1823.

"On Saturday last a man named Feake led his wife into Chipping Ongar market in Essex by a halter, and there exposed her for sale. She was soon purchased by a young man, a blacksmith of High Ongar, at the price of ten shillings. Her person was by no means unpleasing and she appeared to be about 25 years of age. The collector of the tolls actually demanded and received from the purchaser the customary charge of one penny which is always paid upon livestock per head."

George Borrow, describing a similar happening in *Romany Rye* (1857), the sale of Mary Fulcher by her husband, "a drunken quarrelsome fellow," to a horse-dealer for eighteen pence, may have taken this account from the *Times* as his raw material. The same happened again at Epping in 1830 when a workhouse master named Godfrey sold a Mrs. Rudley, possibly one of his inmates, by auction for half a crown and was prosecuted for selling goods and chattels without a licence. The case was dismissed because the wife was not deemed to be the goods and chattels of her husband. It appears from this that the husband was alive and possibly also an inmate separated from his wife, as was the custom in workhouses at that time; therefore he could not have any use for her, neither was she in his possession. She was therefore sold, possibly to help lessen the parish poor rate.

As the article in the *Times* pointed out, the practice was illegal and an indictable offence. At the same time it was quite customary, as magistrates were either ignorant or conniving and it took place in many parts of England. Women's Lib was a sorely needed movement.

Ordeal and Bull-Roarer

Orders of chivalry, priesthood and medicine all had their rites of initiation. A Yoruba of Western Nigeria had to undergo a sound thrashing before he could qualify for kingship. In Mexico a postulant had his nose pierced. A Sioux Indian, before he could become a medicine-man, was bound to the earth nearly naked by cords passed under the skin, and he was compelled, bow and arrows in his hand, to stare at the sun's disc for one whole day.

The Australian aborigine went through a series of tests which included the knocking out of some of his front teeth, tattooing, bloodletting, ceremonial painting of the body, combat, being tossed in the air, having gashes cut and multiple designs of scars made on the front and back of his body, each tribe having its own designs. Only at the end of all these ordeals were the secrets of the tribe laid bare to him and was he allowed to see the sacred *tundun* or bull-roarer and to hear its deep and terrible tones. This was a flat wooden object carved with the patterns belonging to his clan. Through a hole in one end, a string or long piece of hide was passed and it was swung round rapidly to make a loud humming or booming noise.

This was the voice of the Great Spirit, only to be heard by fully initiated members of the tribe.

The Knot

There is a strongly-scented garden plant known by the name of southernwood because of its Mediterranean origin. In olden times a young lover, at a loss for words, often called in its aid, pulling a sprig and presenting it to the girl of his choice. If she smelt it he was accepted; if she threw it away his hopes were dashed. Our common name for the plant is ladslove.

We often talk about the lover's knot though we rarely or never see one. It served, like the plant, as an indication of acceptance or rejection. The young man made two knots of straw, the more ornamental the better, and one of these he presented to his hoped-for sweetheart. If she accepted it and pinned it over her heart they were betrothed and both wore them until their wedding day.

Today betrothal, which amounts to a promise of marriage, means comparatively little for many couples do not even become formally engaged. Neither has the ending of a betrothal much more importance socially, however serious it may be to the two parties concerned, nor is there any longer, as there used to be, a legal breach of promise. At one time betrothal was a necessary preliminary to marriage and today in some parts of the world it still is, and is conducted with considerable ceremony.

Some 50 miles north-east of Amsterdam is the Dutch township of Staphorst, one of the strangest places on earth whose people still belong to the very strictest of all Calvinist sects. They don't read newspapers or magazines, they don't watch television, they use no electricity, modern plumbing or running water, they shun vaccination and refrain from any kind of group entertainments, such as card-playing, dinner parties and dancing. Among the women-folk, cosmetics are banned.

Yet their customs with regard to sex, at least for couples before marriage, might be considered considerably more liberal than ours, however permissive our society may be thought. These customs go back a thousand years to the time when the people were fishermen on the north coasts of the Zuider Zee, later settling on the land to become farmers.

A University of Groningen sociologist reports that a bride cannot be married in their Reformed Association Church *unless* she is pregnant. Thus, Friday evenings are set aside for premarital intercourse between young persons. The way it works is that the father of a marriageable girl erects a heart-shaped copper plate on the front door announcing that his daughter is receiving suitors, then the girl leaves her bedroom "courting-window" open for eligible youths to climb through.

On the other hand, the people deal most harshly with those who break the sixth commandment. Married men or women who commit adultery are put to the ultimate degradation of being paraded in a manure cart through the town bound hand and foot, while people lining the street throw things at them. After that they are blackballed for life.

A custom not quite so bizarre and known as *bundling* was practiced in the British Isles as well as in Holland, Norway and New England. Courting couples were not only allowed, but were expected, to spend a night alone in the girl's bedroom. The difference between this and Staphorst was that in bundling they were supposed to remain fully clothed and separated from each other by layers of bedding. In Holland, an iron vessel and a pair of fire-tongs were left in the room so that if the young man became too ardent, she could sound the alarm. Many a time she did not and a pregnancy resulted. If the baby arrived before the couple were married, the baby, visible to all, was taken to the wedding under its mother's cloak.

Though young men and women today may and do often make arrangements to live together, there is no such thing as an officially recognized trial marriage. Yet in Scotland, one of the strictest of Calvinist countries, trial marriage was widespread. The only necessary ceremony was the verbal pledge given by one to the other before witnesses while holding hands, hence the name *handfasting*. They were then, according to Scottish law, entitled to live together for a year and a day. At Dumfries, young men and women could choose their companions at the annual fair and make the compact, the witness being a priest nicknamed Book-in-the-Bosom because he carried with him the book in which the trial marriages were written down. If, within the prescribed period, it did not work out the erstwhile partners were entitled to go their own ways, the child if any resulting from the partnership being brought up by the party which objected to carrying on the arrangement.

Conjugal Rights

If a stranger to Anglo-Saxon countries were to be asked who, at a wedding, is the best man, he would certainly say, "The bridegroom of course."

In fact it is not so.

Hundreds of years ago in Scotland when a man wanted a wife he chose the girl who took his fancy and he seized her by force. This is rather obviously called marriage by capture. And, since it amounted to kidnapping and the girl's family might well resist, he needed to have around him men who had courage and strength.

So he enlisted the help of his best and most faithful friends.

The trustiest and most valiant one of all came to be known as the best man.

The groom waits nervously in church. The bride is late as usual. Ten minutes after the appointed time she comes down the aisle accompanied by her father or, failing him, whoever is appointed by the family to give her away. She wears part of her trousseau—today her complete outfit—once the *trusse* or bundle of valuables originally paid to the husband. In Balkan countries before the beginning of this century, she was also expected to supply the groom with full sets of underwear made by herself. Over her face she wears the veil, first adopted by the Greeks and the Romans to protect their women from the evil glances of rejected and jealous suitors.

During the ceremony the best man passes over the ring and the bridegroom places it on the bride's third finger which, it was once thought, had a vein which ran directly to the heart, the seat of all emotions. It is made of gold which keeps its value forever and does not rust—a symbol of a long and perfect union.

The ceremony is over, the register signed, the bride and bridegroom leave the church to the sound of the Wedding March. Guests and friends standing at the churchyard gate shower them with rice and confetti, once fertility symbols expressing the hope that they would have a large and happy family.

They go home or to a restaurant where a meal is prepared. In Holland the bridal couple were offered salted cream sprinkled with sugar, for marriage is at times both sweet and bitter. In England the cake contains bitter almonds. Parts of it are given out or sent by post. In Roman times the cake, or bread as it was then, was broken over the head of the bride, again to bring prosperity. To make doubly sure, a bride in Greece on entering her new home crushed a pomegranate, another fertility symbol, and marked the doorpost of the house with a cross in butter.

Nowadays the happy couple embark on a honeymoon. In olden days, honey was recommended as an aphrodisiac, to be taken in plenty during the first month of married life. In Greece, friends would roll a chubby baby over the bridal bed to ensure offspring in plenty. In Southern France, friends would burst into the bridal chamber bringing soup in a chamber-pot which, if drunk, was supposed to achieve the same end.

In feudal England, the married couple were by no means so lucky, for the lord of the manor and not the bridegroom had the customary right of spending the first night after the wedding with the bride. In Madras, India, not only the groom but the whole of his family were considered to have married her and every one of the groom's brothers had the same rights as he had.

If all the omens, symbols, gifts and good wishes mean anything no marriage should fail, but it needs more than these to keep it off the rocks. One is reminded of an old saying of the Amish people of Pennsylvania: "Kissing wears out—cooking don't."

•

Hospitality Gone Mad

You have to keep up with the Joneses. They run a Mercedes; you must have a Rolls Royce. They go to southern France for their holiday; you must choose Bermuda. If you want to be somebody you must spend, spend, spend—at least that's what some people think.

But what would your feelings be if, to prove your wealth and standing you were expected to invite your friends and all comers to a barbecue in your back garden, shower them with expensive gifts, then bring out your valuables—tapestries, Queen Anne furniture, priceless books and pictures and throw them all on the bonfire, smash up your best crockery, your Dresden and your Sèvres and give them the pieces just so that they will think, "Gosh, these people must be worth a mint!"

That is what the Kwakiutl Indians once did.

How this western Canadian custom came about one can only guess. It may have been that in hard times those who were better off gave to the rest. Thus the society came to be sharply divided into the haves and the have-nots. It may be that instead of fighting and scalping, the chiefs found that this was a better and even less costly way of proving one man's superiority over his peers. In this way the giving of presents became a way of life, so much so that if one received a gift from another he found himself bound to give back something of even greater value. One way of humiliating a person you did not like was to give him an expensive present. His inability to return a fitting gift would be a serious blow to his self-respect.

Ostentation such as this was demonstrated at marriage ceremonies, agreements, settlements of disputes and at any other events of importance. At such times one would invite the rest of the community to a potlatch (Chinook *potshatl*—a gift). This was a great feast characterized by eating, drinking and speech-making, followed by the presentation of gifts to all and sundry and the ostentatious destruction of valuables simply to flaunt the wealth of the host. One chief at the end of the 19th century held a potlatch in which a fire was fed with gallons upon gallons of oil and into the blazing inferno were flung seven canoes and 400 blankets among other costly things that could well have been given away to poorer members of the tribe.

At another of these competitive shows of wealth a chief took one of the items Indian tribes valued most of all—a large decorated copper plaque—had it smashed to pieces and divided it between two of his rivals. Not only the plaque but the spirits of the two men were shattered. The first, overcome with surprise and shame, fell dead on the spot; the other, unable to return a gift approaching the value of what he had been given and overcome by the shame to which he had been subjected, shut himself off and lived only six months more in seclusion and misery. By causing them to lose face, the chief had killed his two rivals as surely as if they had been tomahawked in battle.

Many centuries before, Emperor Flavius of Rome had the same idea of demonstrating his riches and power by an ostentatious display of extravagance.

He invited the noble folk of Rome to a sumptuous feast, each course served on golden plates encrusted with precious stones. To the utter astonishment of the guests he arose at the end of each course and flung his empty plate into the Tiber flowing alongside his villa, bidding his guests to follow suit.

At the end of the evening over 700 gold plates had splashed into the dark waters. What he did not tell the guests, however, was that he had arranged for his servants to suspend nets across the river just below the surface of the water. When the revellers had all gone home, his servants hauled up the nets and recovered his valuables!

However sumptuous the feasts of the Kwakiutl Indians and the Emperors may have been, they could hardly equal in originality and elaboration the fare presented by some nomadic Arab tribesmen to their guests. A sample dish consisted of eggs which were stuffed in fish, the fish then stuffed in chickens, the chickens stuffed in sheep and the sheep finally stuffed in a whole camel, all roasted over a large slow fire.

It is considered good manners among Arabs to express appreciation of a hearty meal by long, deep and sonorous belching. Little effort would be needed after such a spread as this!

Touched for the Evil

In the early days of July 1660, London was a place of pilgrimage, thousands of visitors flocking in—gentry and rich commoners from the provinces, poor parishioners from all the countryside around the capital on horseback, in carts and on foot, some alone, others in small parties, all converging on St. James's Palace for one particular purpose, to be touched for the Evil.

The Evil, as it was called, was scrofula, a form of tuberculosis, for which it was believed that the Royal Touch would bring about a cure. The custom in England was believed to go back as far as the days of Edward the Confessor and in France, the only other country where it was practiced, to a good many years before.

Most English monarchs carried on the ceremony which consisted of the king personally washing the diseased flesh with water, but under the reign of Henry VII (1485–1509) the ablution was omitted and a regular healing through touch service was substituted.

Such a ceremony as this was very useful to a king who was in need of popular support. It helped create an image and Charles II, who needed popular acclaim badly, is stated on good authority to have touched 100,000 such cases. On touching days the rich in their finery, the poor in their rags all took their turns in coming before the King. The diarist John Evelyn saw the ceremony on the 6th of July, 1660 and his graphic eye-witness account cannot be bettered. It is here given in modern spelling:

"His Majesty first began to touch for the Evil according to custom thus: His Majesty sitting under his State in the Banqueting House, the Surgeons cause the sick to be brought or led up to the throne, where they kneeling the King strokes their faces or cheeks with both his hands at once, at which instant the chaplain in his formalities says, 'He put his hands upon them and healed them.'

"This is said to every one in particular. When they have all been touched they come up again in the same order and the other chaplain kneeling, and having angel gold (golden coins marked with the figure of the Archangel Michael and worth approximately 50p or $1 each) strung on white ribbon on his arm, delivers them one by one to His Majesty who puts them about the necks of the touched as they pass whilst the first chaplain repeats 'That is the true light who came into the world.' Then follows the epistle with the liturgy, prayers for the sick . . . lastly the blessing; and the Lord Chamberlain and Controller of the Household bring a basin, ewer and towel for His Majesty to wash."

King Charles evidently took a good deal of trouble over the business and incidentally ran considerable risk of infection from some of his none-too-clean visitors. Though William of Orange refused to touch, referring all requests to the exiled James II at St. Germain, France, the last monarch to carry on the practice, Queen Anne, held frequent sessions. Dr. Samuel Johnson when only 2½ years old was taken by his mother from their home in Chesterfield to London to be touched by Her Majesty.

"The touch, however," says Johnson's biographer Boswell, "was without any effect."

Woman and Child

Many superstitions and customs are focused on the woman. The male has never quite been able to understand her. In some primitive societies neither he nor she, for instance, realized why she became pregnant, a fact which seems strange and almost unbelievable to us.

This arises partly from the treatment of women not as human beings but as property to be employed like other property, in cementing friendships, working out agreements, completing business and other transactions.

Take again the example of the Australian aborigines. The male members of the tribe before an expedition to take revenge on a nearby tribe would temporarily exchange wives with each other as a token of unity and friendship. When one party was about to attack another, the latter if it did not want to fight, would send a certain number of women to the former. If they wished to make a treaty they would have sexual intercourse with them; if not they would send them back untouched. When a conflict was ended, the making of peace almost invariably involved the temporary exchange of women between erstwhile enemies.

Among primitive peoples, it is perhaps not to be wondered at that intercourse and paternity are not thought of as being connected. Even in places where it was recognized that man had something to do with the production of children, it was still thought that the real power behind conception was out of his control.

Much more pitiful was the case of the woman who, like Rachel in the Old Testament, failed to conceive, and much greater the joy when it happened. Every manner of means—eating, frequenting the company of a pregnant woman or young mother, sitting on her seat or lying on her bed—all these were taken to help to bring about pregnancy.

In tribal life many strange customs are connected with childbirth—the shutting up of women during pregnancy and the varying periods of seclusion imposed on a woman after confinement, the concern about protecting her and the child from the Evil Eye, such as the removal of mirrors from her apartment, the placing of a knife under her bed or pillow as a protection against evil spirits, and the tragedy in the rejection from society of the woman whose newborn child has died.

The onset of puberty is especially dangerous for both sexes, but especially for women, and many strange customs have grown up to protect them. Young girls in some parts of the world are still kept in seclusion for months after the first onset of menstruation; they may not see the sun, touch the ground or eat certain foods. Grown women may not look on initiation rites or approach the men's clubhouse; in some cases they are even forbidden to eat with their husbands. Over large regions of the world religion and custom decree that women be veiled. In Japan before Westernization, if a woman was caught alone with a man who was not her husband, she was immediately put to death, even if the meeting was completely innocent.

There still remain in England superstitions concerning the preservation of the caul or amnion, the sac containing the human embryo which is sometimes found remaining round the head of a child at birth. The Scots call it *sely how* or lucky hood. A child born with it about the head was destined to be fortunate for life, and sailors would buy the hoods to take on voyages as charms to ensure safe journeys. A mother would present one to her daughter on her marriage saying, "Keep this and you will always have a home; lose it and you will be unsettled for life." This family treasure, for such it is in some homes, is in appearance like a dry, thin yellowish piece of plastic and is stored away in many a secret drawer.

In the Chinese written language the ideograph that stands for trouble represents two women under the same roof, and there is still one place in the world where anything female is taboo. This is the Greek monastery of Mount Athos where males have been isolated for more than 700 years. Men may enter, but no women; roosters but no hens; horses but no mares; bulls but no cows. The environs are actually patrolled by armed guards to make certain that nothing feminine passes through the gates.

Mihailo Tolotos, a monk of Mount Athos who died in 1938 at the age of 82, was probably the only man never to have laid eyes on a woman. His mother died when he was born and on the following day he was taken to the monastery where he spent the remainder of his life and never left it, even for a short time.

Fashion and Fad

As far as fashion is concerned neither sex can be said to be more or less ridiculous than the other.

"Yankee* doodle went to town
Riding on a pony;
Put a feather in his hat
And called it Macaroni."

The Macaronis of the 1760's and 1770's had probably the most extravagantly ridiculous clothes and hair-dos ever known—great masses of macaroni-like artificial hair piled up on the head, tiny hats, clothes of the richest materials fitting close to the body, long walking-sticks adorned with tassels or ribbons. Their etiquette matched their dress, foppish and superficial. The women could even outdo the men with enormous headdresses fixed on frames of wire and bearing all kinds of ornaments—nests, bowls of fruit and such. These ornaments were both unclean and uncomfortable. The woman's headdress was said to be capable of accommodating, and sometimes did, a family of mice. Other unpleasant creatures also found homes there.

Sometimes, however, old customs seemingly bizarre and senseless can be proven by modern research to have validity. Thus pirates in the olden days, and women even up to the

---

* The term *Yankee* is believed to have been taken by the Indians from the French settlers in America who referred to the Englishman as l'Anglais. The native Americans in turn adopted the corruption and it was applied during the Civil War to the northern soldiers, and after that to all inhabitants of the northern U.S., especially New Englanders.

Another suggestion is that it comes from the Dutch Jankin (young John) or Jan Kees (John Cornelius).

present, have been accustomed to pierce the lobe of the ear and wear earrings, often under the impression that the pierced ear was an aid to good sight. This has been ridiculed until recently, but in these days of acupuncture and other forms of fringe medicine, evidence is mounting that it may work. Whatever the truth of this may be, there is not yet any justification for the fashion of elegant English women in the late 19th century of wearing gold rings through their nipples.

In an 1899 edition of the British journal *Society*, fascinating details are given about this particular fad. The woman who wished to wear such ornaments, the magazine said, had holes bored through her nipples and thin golden rings threaded through the holes. It was believed that wearing such rings made the breasts fuller and rounder, and that the rings, when exposed, were a stimulating sight for men. The operation was performed, not by doctors, but by jewellers much in the same way as ear-piercing is done today.

Personal vanity is a world-wide phenomenon. A good set of one's own pearly-white teeth is something to be proud of, but in medieval Japan fashionable women either blackened or gilded their teeth. Even in Britain a gold filling in a front tooth may be regarded as an asset rather than a disadvantage, possibly because gold is associated with wealth and prestige, and there is no limit to the extremes people will go to on that account. Today many Hindu women stain their teeth bright red to enhance their appearance while some African tribes file them to points. The Maya Indians of South America did this so that they could fill the cavities with precious gems and jade.

Vain Man!

Men were no less vain. In Spain from the 14th century onwards the beard was considered to be a sign of manhood and virility, the bigger and more expansive the better. Drake's metaphor about singeing the King of Spain's beard had some basis in reality. Woe to the wretch who had a weedy, limp growth! He had to have recourse to the false beard, and soon the whole of the Spanish fashion world was imitating him, while many quite substantial beards were shaved off to accommodate the false monsters.

In the morning a grandee dandy would drape his chin in a crimson beard, in the evening he would serenade his senorita in an adjustable long black appendage, and he could don what size or shade he fancied for other occasions, as we today choose shirts or ties. Well might Bottom in Shakespeare's *Midsummer Night's Dream* talk about "your straw-colour beard, your orange-tawny beard, your purple-in-grain beard, or your French crown colour beard, your perfect yellow." They were all at hand for the man who had the money.

The trouble was that when they were donned nobody knew who was who, and soon Spanish society was resembling nothing short of a general masquerade party. Creditors could not catch up with debtors; the police arrested the innocent while villains hid behind vast growths of hair. Wives attached themselves with dire consequences to the wrong husbands and the price of horse-hair rocketed. In the end, Peter IV of Aragon had to put a stop to the farce by prohibiting the wearing of false beards.

Not only in Spain, but in England too, at the turn of this century a beard was something to be proud of, witness the following advertisements appearing in a journal of the day:

"BEARDS! BEARDS! BEARDS! VOLOSCI, the only hair-growing specific, one shilling for three boxes.

"MOUSTACHES. Why is one young man able to grow a luxuriant moustache at 18 or even younger and another can't show any hair on his face at perhaps 26? GRENADIER, the hair-root stimulant one shilling a box. Despatched in plain cover."

It was often the royal personage who indulged in what seem to us the most extravagant and ridiculous eccentricities. It was customary for Louis XIV of France to allow privileged persons to enter the bedroom of the King and Queen in the morning and to witness the most intimate details of breakfasting, rising and being dressed. Anybody who wished to gain admission to the royal bedroom did not knock but was expected to scratch with the fingernail on the door.

When King Louis and his Queen Marie-Thérèse were

awakened in the morning, if the Queen sat up after the curtains of the bed had been drawn and clapped her hands the servants knew that the King had performed his royal duty the night before—intercourse with the Queen! "O tempora, o mores!"

The eccentricities of the queens of 17th century China extended even to the treatment of their Pekingese dogs which were considered sacred. At the court of Li Hsui, one of the last queens of the Manchu dynasty, every Pekingese dog had its own human wetnurse and its own eunuch to protect it from other dogs. Some dogs even had private palaces complete with staffs of servants.

The Last Act

Any visitor taking a closer look at some of the English country churchyards may notice that the oldest and best preserved graves are usually on the south side for, when village population was small and there was plenty of room for the dead, that was the popular side of the church, and here the gentry erected their elaborate memorials. Those who had led saintly lives, often members of the clergy, were laid to rest on the eastern side because it faced the Holy Land, while commoners and poorer villagers usually had graves to the west of the church.

Tombstones had a fourfold purpose—to mark the grave so that the place could be recognized, to consign the dead to the care of the gods, to make sure that the body of the deceased would not be disturbed and that the spirit would not rise again and trouble the living. In this last case, relatives of those buried on the south side would think themselves far less likely to be visited by the ghosts of their ancestors.

Nobody liked the north. The old Scandinavian region of *Hela* from which we get our word "hell" and to which cowards were consigned, was to the northern peoples no inferno such as Dante represented it but a place of darkness, ice and snow—a fit place for wrongdoers. It was on this side of the church that criminals and sometimes paupers were interred. Today when we have more living and more dead, even that space too has been filled.

In previous times some members of the community were not considered fit to have graves within the churchyard at all. A legend of St. Sigfrid tells how the murderers of his sister's sons were doomed "to have the feet of their dead bodies bound with ropes, to be dragged to the place where the wild beast dwelt and where the sun could not penetrate, and to have a great heap of stones cast over them."

In England until 1824 when the law was changed, many suicides and some criminals were buried outside the churchyard altogether and their remains even today are sometimes dug up when construction work is being done. This happened recently on a main road near to a town where several skeletons were unearthed. Not one of them had any hands!

The usual place for burying suicides was where roads met, and it was customary to drive a stake through the body. This was because it was believed that the ghosts of those buried outside the churchyard would return and plague the living unless they were "pinned down." Thomas Hood in one of his humorous ballads tells how Ben Battle, an ex-soldier, hanged himself for love of faithless Nelly Gray and how an inquest was held over him by a coroner's jury:

"A dozen men sat on his corpse
To find out why he died—
And they buried him at the crossroads
With a stake in his inside!"

BIZARRE WEATHER

The Moon Rainbow and the Comet
Fire from Heaven
Pictures Etched by Lightning
The Boggart
Cloud Pictures
Spectral Armies and Cities
Things That Go Bang
The Somerset Bumps
Strange Hailstorms
Stone Falls
Peculiar Showers
"If It's Up There . . ."

BIZARRE WEATHER

The Moon Rainbow and the Comet

There are few natural features more fascinating than the rainbow. You walk towards it, it retreats. You go away from it, it follows you. On level country you see it in the far distance; where there are hills, woods or buildings the lower arcs interpose themselves, giving coloration to grass and trees or adding variegated lines to blank walls. Try as you may, you will never catch it.

In a German lesson a long time ago, the pupils were reading aloud from Schiller's play *William Tell* while the master explained the meaning of the words and phrases. They had reached the scene in which Tell, Fürst and Stauffacher, the leaders of the people of the three cantons, met their followers in a meadow called the Rütli and all took an oath that they would not cease fighting until they had freed their land from the tyranny of Emperor Rudolf and his henchman Gessler. It was night-time, and they gathered under a full moon which hung in the southern sky and facing it in the north was the wide arch of a double moon rainbow.

A double moon rainbow! Surely there couldn't be such a thing. In the bright sunlight certainly, we'd all seen one, but at night . . . !

"Yes," said the master, "they do appear but they are very rare. I doubt if you'll ever see one as long as you live."

I did within a few months. There, just as on the Rütli meadow so long ago, was the same full moon which shone under the rain clouds, a grey sky opposite, cut by two almost semicircular bands of red and green light, much fainter in the outer band than the inner one, and between them a sky darker than the rest as if the light had been withdrawn from it to enhance the effect of the two variegated arcs.

Next morning at school no eyebrows were raised at my particular experience, and in fact though the German master was encouraging, half the class refused to believe the story. But why indeed should they? They hadn't seen it, for they all lived some six miles from my home. The double moon rainbow was my own special visitation and I was glad of it.

We go back farther to the year 1910, the year of the comet. It was first spotted by an astronomer in Leipzig in September, 1909, and from that month onward night after night it came nearer and nearer, a brilliant greenish-white head and a wide-curving luminous tail arching itself over the southern sky.

People took fright. Some said it was bound to hit the earth, others that it was an omen presaging evil happenings. At night, we stood in the street in groups staring and speculating.

In school, the teacher tried her best to explain what a comet was. She told us that nobody need be afraid, for the comet's tail was made up of millions and millions of tiny particles mixed up with luminous gases and none of them would ever hit the surface of the earth; in fact if we passed clean through the comet's tail not one of us would know unless the scientists told us.

We believed her and learnedly tried to still the forebodings of the more ignorant.

But wasn't it true that the visitations of comets brought disaster? The teacher showed us a picture of the Bayeux tapestry on which the same comet appeared. Surely the battle of Hastings which followed its visitation was a disaster for Harold and England? Maybe it was, but William the Conqueror came well out of it and the comet was as much French as English.

It is due back again in 1986, so look out!

The double moon rainbow and Halley's comet are perfectly well explained by those who know all about these things, but to one schoolboy and to thousands who might have seen them they were bizarre enough incidents to be remembered for a lifetime.

Fire from Heaven

Ever since Benjamin Franklin flew his kite, it has been known that lightning is an electrical phenomenon and nobody can account for the strange way in which it sometimes behaves. We know, for instance, how dangerous it is to stand under an isolated tree or in the open during a thunderstorm and why parents tell their children to keep away from doors, fireplaces and windows; but why should an oak tree be fifty times more liable to be struck than a beech, and why should loam, which is a mixture of clay, sand and organic matter, attract lightning some twenty times as readily as chalk?

Lightning sometimes comes when it is least expected. On a sunny day when there is not a cloud in the sky the whole earth can be shaken by a deafening crack followed by a roar, and felt more violently than in any violent storm of rain for the simple reason that it comes so suddenly. That's why we call it a bolt from the blue. In 1893, a troop of 19 French soldiers were on the march near Bourges in cloudless weather when, according to a reliable account, they were struck "by an unknown force." All were thrown to the ground and some were killed.

This force is what the ancients called Jove's thunderbolt, whose victims in ancient Greece, Etruria and Rome were not given the normal burial rites. In Rome, by a law of King Numa Pompilius, they were not to be burnt according to the prevalent custom of disposing of the dead, but buried.

We can understand why certain localities, perhaps because of the kind of soil, their proximity to water or their height above sea level may attract lightning. The Romans regarded these places as sacred, made sacrifices there and fenced them off, while the Etruscans built temples on the spots. Some prehistoric sites in Britain, such as the Rollright Stones in Oxfordshire, are believed to have been places where thunderbolts or meteorites have once fallen.

But why should certain people attract lightning even to the extent of being struck seven times—and survive? Nobody knows.*

In 1918, a certain Major Summerford was wounded in the First World War, not by a bullet or a fragment of shell but by a lightning stroke which paralyzed him temporarily from the waist down. Six years later while he was fishing in Vancouver lightning again struck the tree under which he sat, paralyzing him, permanently this time, all down the right side.

Pictures Etched by Lightning

In June, 1896, two workmen near Marseilles were sheltering in a hut from a thunderstorm when it was struck. They were both thrown to the ground and parts of their clothing were torn off. On the skin of one of the workmen was found the shape of a pine tree, a poplar and the handle of the workman's watch. How the representations were etched on the man's skin by lightning remains a puzzle. True, there were pines and poplars within viewing distance but nobody could give any reason why one of each was chosen and why such an obscure thing as a watch-handle should have appeared.

Strange stories of this kind abound, some probably true, others about which there is a great deal of doubt. The word *keranography* does not appear in any of our smaller English dictionaries. Yet the imprinting of representations of objects on other objects struck by lightning was the subject of a lecture to the British Association in 1863 in which the speaker mentioned how a young girl was standing by a window outside

---

* Roy Sullivan, of Virginia, a forest ranger, has been verified by the editors of the *Guinness Book of World Records* as having been struck seven times.

of which was a maple, and how as a result of a lightning-stroke the image of the tree appeared on her body.

Such imprints as these are even reported to have been made by lightning beneath the skin as when in 1812 at Combe Hay, Somerset, England, six sheep were struck and imprints of the scene around, including an adjacent oak wood, were found on the *inside* of the hides. In 1971, Mrs. Jasper Barnett, skinning a rabbit shot by her husband found on the flesh of one of its forelegs the representation of a woman's face with a rosebud mouth, curly hair and long eyelashes.

Such stories may appear tall enough to be unbelievable, but are vouched for by eminent scientists including the distinguished French professor Camille Flammarion who conjectured that the skin acts as a sort of camera and the lightning as the flash. This could well be so, except that there is nothing which could function as a lens, no possibility of focusing nor does the explanation account for the pictures being only of selected parts of the surroundings—a tree, a face, a watch-handle, or a nail. Moreover, many of the stories relate to the distant past and for some of them there are no living witnesses.

The Boggart

There are three kinds of lightning: one is sheet lightning which we see as an all-over flash in one part of the sky followed by a roll of thunder some seconds later. At such times the storm is quite a distance away and we can estimate this by counting the seconds between the flash and the beginning of the roll, figuring five seconds to the mile. As the storm comes nearer the lightning becomes more visible and we can see it as a fork. The point or points where it strikes the earth can be plainly seen and the clap of thunder immediately following is succeeded by a loud roar.

In addition to these two, there is a third kind which, though light-producing, is not of the same nature as sheet or fork lightning. It is generally known as ball lightning and appears as fireballs, things of which we have all heard but few of us have ever seen. Indoors it is known as wildfire in some districts, and outdoors as will-o'-the-wisp, jack o' lantern, corpse candles or the boggart.

An electronics engineer named Robert Burch was looking in his mirror when he saw coming through the open window of the Bremerton, Washington, Y.M.C.A. room where he was staying, an orange-red ball of fire. He was just in time to step out of its way when it burst with a blinding flash and a deafening noise. Luggage and two radio sets were badly burnt and Burch, his right arm injured, was taken off to hospital.[1]

A young girl was seated at a table when she noticed a large ball of fire moving slowly across the room in her direction. It then darted towards a hole in the chimney and climbed up it. On reaching the open air it exploded just above the roof with a crash that shook the entire house.[2]

Both these happenings are well authenticated.

These floating balls of fire, though very terrifying, do not for the most part appear to be injurious and, even in a room, they normally seem to avoid coming into contact with people as in the case of the young girl. But if touched or kicked, their equilibrium appears to be affected and they are liable to explode, doing considerable damage.

In the open air they may be seen at night, especially near level and marshy ground and around churchyards. Hence their association with death. On one occasion, passengers in a coach from Llandeilo to Carmarthen in Wales saw three of these "corpse candles" as they crossed a bridge over a river. A few days later three men were in a boat on the river below when it capsized and all three were drowned. The Rev. Sabine Baring-Gould, folklore expert and author of *Onward Christian Soldiers*, writes about the floating lights accompanying coffins to the grave or hovering over newly-made graves in a churchyard. On lonely roads they were reputed to attract wayfarers who took them for the lights in cottage windows, to their deaths in the bogs. Hence the name *boggart* given to them in the North Country.

---

[1] Michael Harrison, *Fire from Heaven.*

[2] Frank Lane, *The Elements Rage.*

Thus we go back to the marsh, which has both moisture and decaying matter, the chemical reaction within it liberating methane or marsh gas, and this may be an element in these floating balls of light, though even now the reason why they move is still obscure. Out of doors they take various forms and are associated in folklore with fairies and little people. But it is as the will-o'-the-wisp, mentioned by the Victorian ballad-singer that we best know them:

"I dance, I dance, I'm here, I'm there;
Who tried to catch me catches but air.
The mortal who follows me follows in vain,
For I laugh, ha ha!
I laugh, ho ho!
I laugh at their folly and pain."

Cloud Pictures

"And the Lord went before them by day in a pillar of a cloud to lead them in the way; and by night in a pillar of fire, to give them light to go by day and night." (Exodus 13: 21)

The journey of the Israelites to the Promised Land is one of the earliest accounts of the weather aiding the purposes of man, guiding the tribes to the crossing-point of the Red Sea, then moving behind them to cover the Egyptian armies with a dark mist, while the Israelites, the sea having parted, went through.

A modern parallel may be drawn from the story of a British naval officer during the Allied invasion of North Africa in the Second World War. There was a calm sea and a clear sky which left the whole fleet an easy target for enemy bombers. Not for long, however, for before any advantage could be taken of the situation, an immense black cloud came over, settling on the entire fleet and remaining there for ten consecutive days.

We can have cloud pictures, pictures in the fire, pictures in the design of patterned wallpaper, pictures in anything when there is depth or contrast in coloration as in trees or rock formations. Some are so near to reality as to be uncanny; others have to be assisted by the imagination. During a bombing mission in the Korean War a cameraman photographed a giant Christ-figure in the clouds, holding up the right arm as if giving a blessing. Much the same features, but the face only, were caught by another camera on an aircraft, this time in the Alps, etched in the melting snow on the side of a mountain.

Odd shapes, such as these in clouds and mists, have often been the background or even the material of religious apparitions and visions. In 1964, Signora Quattrini, known locally as Mamma Rosa, was talking to a friend in an orchard in San Damiano, Italy, when a cloud overhead moved behind one of the trees where it gradually assumed the shape of a woman on whose head a crown appeared, and in each hand a flower. This was the first of a number of visions of the Virgin seen by the Signora, but it is said that nobody else saw them.

Spectral Armies and Cities

Not only single figures, but armies, ships, trees and towns are reported to have been seen in the sky. The most common of these sightings is the mirage, described as an optical illusion by which oases and lakes appear in arid deserts, icebergs and ships on the sea and in polar regions. These have sometimes been seen inverted or suspended in the atmosphere.

In 1909, the explorer Robert Peary on his journey to the North Pole sighted a mountain range. Four years later Donald MacMillan set out to find and explore it. But, as his party moved forward to reach the range it retreated before them, and then as the sun sank it disappeared completely. What Peary had seen was a mirage caused by rays of light curved or refracted by differences of temperature in the atmosphere.

It is hard to see how refracted light could transport the image of a whole city halfway across the world, but this has happened. Bristol in England has frequently been seen in the sky over parts of Alaska, especially during the months of June and July. The explorer Hugh L. Willoughby claimed to have seen and photographed it in 1887. He actually produced the print which was so accurate that many believed it to be a fake. Others who saw the mirages said the outlines of the city were more like Toronto, Montreal and even Peking, but, whatever it might have been, it was certainly out of the ordinary. Much later during the First World War a German submarine commander, peering through the glass of his periscope saw, not a British ship but the complete silhouette of New York City in the distance—this though the submarine was far out in the mid-Atlantic.

Much more difficult to explain are the phantom armies which have appeared at various periods in history. The most recent sighting of all was in November, 1956, when two men camping in the Cuillin Mountains of Skye were terrified at about 3 o'clock in the morning at the sight of dozens of kilted Highlanders charging across the stony ground. The next evening while they were in camp higher up the mountain at almost the same time they saw the same vision, but this time the Highlanders appeared to be retreating across the boulders looking weary and half-dead.

So far nobody has been able to explain these "moving mirages" if this is what they are. Charles Fort, the writer and collector of records of unusual happenings, says: "There has never been an explanation that does not itself have to be explained."

Things That Go Bang

At ten in the morning of the 2nd of December, 1977, the winter calm above South Carolina's tourist beaches was shattered by a blast so loud that scientists said it could have taken 100 tons of dynamite to duplicate it if it were heard from a distance of 50 miles from the shore.

It was a cool day with no sign of a storm, but people heard this shatteringly loud noise followed by a rumbling like thunder, coupled with a tremor which had the same effect as a high-intensity explosion in the atmosphere.

At 3:45 p.m. on the same day and a few hundred miles north on the New Jersey shore a similar boom came out of the Atlantic skies toppling knickknacks from the shelves of houses and breaking windows. Employees at the Oyster Creek nuclear plant in New Jersey were evacuated, fearing there might have been an earth tremor, but officials of the Columbia University Lamont Laboratory across the Hudson ruled it out. "It's possibly some secret equipment," said the Director of Acoustics Research. There were other explanations—that these high-altitude explosions, none of them nuclear, might be connected with the Pentagon's efforts to develop a killer satellite to counter the one which the Russians already possessed.

The whole Atlantic coast was later disturbed by further explosions, the major ones on the 15th, 20th, 22nd and 24th, causing earthquake needles as far away as 50 miles inland to jump wildly. Early in the morning of the 23rd the police and officials in New Canaan, Connecticut, received repeated calls reporting three explosions accompanied by flashes of red light. The fire department sent out engines but found no damage. "From the calls we received we expected to see a house blown off its foundations," said one official.

At the same time Ted Weeks, a fisherman at Barnegat Light on the New Jersey coastline heard one which shook the whole house. "Almost immediately," he said, "the second report followed but not near as loud. It was very distinct. The whole of Long Beach Island I'm sure must have heard it. You had to be dead not to have heard it."

People as far north as Nova Scotia in Canada were mystified by the booms, which were clearly heard by all the 1,500 inhabitants of the seashore hamlet of Barrington near the southern tip of the peninsula. An airline pilot told federal officials that he had seen a flash of green light in the afternoon sky on the 2nd of December.

Though all these explosions had disturbed seismographs, they were by this time acknowledged not to have been caused by earthquakes but rather, as some called them, "airquakes."

President Carter, alarmed by reports from almost the whole of the east coast, on December 29th ordered top governmental agencies to investigate and report. They could come up with nothing. "We have no knowledge or explanation for any of the reported explosions," said the Defense Department. The Coast Guard could not add to the comment. The National Aeronautics and Space Administration (NASA) said, "We don't know anything about them and don't have any explanation for them at this time." The Geological Survey said they *couldn't* be explained; the Department of the Interior could do no more than quote what the Geological Survey had said. Nobody was any the wiser.

At the same time similar bangs were being heard in the southwestern counties of England, none of them fitting in with the timetables of the Concorde flights by either British Airways or Air France. They could not therefore be caused by supersonic flight. They had been strong enough to rock lookout posts at Gwennap Head and St. Just in Cornwall. Coast Guard Peter Baker at first suspected gunfire but the Joint Service Coordination Centre at Plymouth reported none. No flares had been fired by coast guards, there was no freak weather nor any blasting connected with oil rigs. It all seemed a complete mystery.

Various explanations were put forward by unofficial bodies. The most ingenious one was that the explosions had been caused by gas bubbling up from underwater dumps where garbage from coastal cities had been sunk. Dr. Stanley Klemetson, environmental engineering researcher and Associate Professor of Civil Engineering at Colorado State University, explained that it was likely that the build-up of sludge deposits on the ocean bottom from the dumping of treated organic wastes and garbage had produced gases such as hydrogen and methane. As these had accumulated beneath the sludge, sufficient quantity of the liberated gases could break through the layer and rise to the surface of the ocean. Being warmer than the air they could rise into the atmosphere and be ignited by static electricity caused by wind friction. It was ingenious but unlikely.

Another theory was that the bangs presaged earthquake activity and a third was the inevitable speculation that beings from other planets had had a hand in them. All these had to be abandoned. All one could say was that they arose from a combination of different causes. What these were nobody seemed to know.

"It is," said one expert, "a physical phenomenon we don't understand. These noises are in a class of their own."

The Somerset Bumps

Bangs similar to those on the North American coast had been heard for several months in England. At the end of 1976, Mr. George Lawrence of North Petherton, Somerset, had been annoyed by overhead noises which were so intense as to shake his house round about 9 o'clock every evening. On his reporting the nuisance some 600 people sent letters to Bristol University saying that they too had heard the noises.

An investigation followed. At that time there was a good deal of concern about the sonic booms made by Concorde and most people thought this new aircraft was the source of the "Somerset Bump." The scientists, while not denying the assertion, and anxious not to be thought either pro- or anti-Concorde played down the nuisance. Dr. Tom Lawson, a reader in industrial aerodynamics, described the bang as equivalent to no more than the slamming of a car door 50 yards away. Others said that the bangs could normally be heard only with the aid of sophisticated equipment or by people "living in a couple of acres in the middle of the country with only hens for company."

Their explanation was that the sound was not the actual sonic boom made by Concorde, but was "rebound or secondary bump" brought about by the refraction of sound waves caused by gradients of wind and temperature at heights of up to 25 miles in the stratosphere. Concorde, like all supersonic planes, has this primary double boom when the sound travels downward, but under certain conditions which occur between September and April the waves may be "bent" high in the stratosphere 30 to 60 miles above the ground. The bending appears to be caused by strong winds and a reversal of the normal temperature gradient.

This sort of phenomenon, it was explained, had happened before, not from aircraft but from distant gunfire. Take the entry in the diary of Samuel Pepys for June 4th, 1666, at the time of the sea battle going on between English and Dutch ships off the North Foreland. At the time, he was walking with a friend in St. James's Park, London, where

> "we saw hundreds of people listening at the gravel-pits . . . to hear the guns, and . . . it is a miraculous thing that we all Friday and Saturday and yesterday did hear everywhere most plainly the guns go off, and yet at Deal and Dover to last night they did not hear one word of a fight nor think they heard one gun. This . . . makes room for a great dispute in philosophy, how we should hear it and they not, the same wind that brought it to us being the same that should bring it to them, but so it is."

Similarly, during the First World War, people in Kent could hear the thunder of guns on the Western Front while soldiers nearer the action could not.

Pepys knew nothing about the logical explanation—the bending of sound waves. We in the 20th century have got at least that much farther.

Strange Hailstorms

Joshua during the conquest of Canaan had to meet the five kings of the Amorites in battle. He defeated them at Gibeon when, as he was pursuing the fleeing armies, "the Lord cast down great stones from heaven upon them . . . and they died; they were more which died with hailstones than they whom the children of Israel slew with the sword." (Joshua 10: 11)

We know that hailstones before they fall can grow in the upper atmosphere, and as they drop, accumulate more ice until when they reach the ground they may be large enough to kill living beings. Texas in 1877 suffered a bombardment of hailstones which killed thousands of sheep, and in 1950 a farm in

North Molton in Devonshire was found after a hailstorm to be littered with lumps of ice as large as dinner plates.

On July 4th, 1953, in Long Beach, California, ice chunks weighing more than 50 pounds fell on American Avenue. Two parked cars were struck and damaged, and many bystanders were scared though nobody was hit. Since some of the chunks were vaguely conical it was suggested that they had fallen from a plane, but it was pointed out that such a heavily-iced plane would not have been able to stay in the air, and in any case the ice could not have fallen in the same area over such a long interval of time from a plane flying at normal speed.

Single pieces of falling ice have been even larger. On the 13th of August, 1849, an irregular-shaped block fell at Ord, Ross-shire, measuring 20 feet round and weighing *nearly half a ton*, and in 1951 in Dusseldorf a man working on top of a house was skewered by a huge splinter of ice 6 feet long and 6 inches in diameter.

Explanations have been attempted as to how such enormous weight and bulk manages to stay aloft while growing. Some suggest that strong winds in the upper atmosphere may help pieces to grow while preventing their fall, others that they could be ice meteorites. These may originally have been part of the outer crust of a meteor flicked off as it suddenly heats up on contact with the earth's atmosphere. This part cools, e.g. gathers ice and eventually falls as a giant hailstone.

But why hailstones should take on recognizable shapes is a mystery. This happened on the 12th of June, 1908, at Remire-mont in the Vosges area of eastern France when large, almost spherical hailstones fell, all bearing almost identical prints of a female figure with a robe turned up at the bottom like a priest's robe. These, which fell on an area of land some 440 yards wide and several miles in length, did little damage to crops and came down gently, as if they had been dropped from no more than a few yards. It was believed by devout people that they had fallen because, a week earlier during the feast of the virgin, the town council had prohibited the holding of a procession; therefore this, "a vertical procession," was cast down on the town by the artillery of heaven, each stone bearing a representation of Our

Lady—a fitting answer. The fall of the hailstones was vouched for by no fewer than 107 witnesses.

Stone Falls

Meteorites are made up of stone and metal in various forms, and have certainly at times fallen in showers from the sky. At 2:30 on the morning of the 4th of September, 1886, a shower of stones fell and bounced off the pavement in front of a newspaper office in Charleston, South Carolina. Other showers followed at 7:30 a.m. and 1:30 p.m., and when picked up the stones were found to be warm. The whole area covered was no more than about 75 square feet.

Some of these showers and falls of single stones have shown an unaccountable tendency to pick out certain places and persons. The target of three stone-storms in May, 1921, was a single house in Truro, Cornwall. On the 29th of May, 1922, the target was a chemist's shop in Johannesburg, South Africa, when it was thought that they were "attracted," if such a term can be used, by a native girl who worked there. Even as the police watched, the stones fell vertically from the sky all around her without the girl being touched or hurt.

In October, 1973, two men out fishing in a lake at Skaneateles, New York, had a similar experience. A large stone and then two more larger still fell near them. As they packed up their gear to drive off, more fell. Later when they stopped to change their clothes and again when they called in a bar for a drink they were pelted by other showers. As one left his friend outside his home, a fiercer shower than ever rattled all round them.

Thus we seem to proceed from the normal, the meteorite, to the paranormal, the unaccountable rain of rock which seems to be able to fall, as the Bible puts it, "where it listeth."

Strange substances have fallen from the sky at times—salt crystals, copper alloy, clinkers, alabaster, carbonate of soda, glass and metallic fragments of all kinds. They could not all have been dropped by aircraft as planes capable of dropping them hardly existed before 1914. One bizarre incident, however, did concern aircraft.

Mr. and Mrs. Chris Elkins of Addlestone, Surrey, England, were surprised one day when a large lump of ice fell on to their lawn, denting it badly. They informed the police who took it away and stored it in their refrigerator until they realized what it was—a block of frozen urine jettisoned from a passing aircraft.

Somewhere in the world there is a jet air-liner which had a leaky lavatory system.

Peculiar Showers

Well may people look up at the sky when such things happen and murmur, "Why pick me?"

In July, 1955, Ed Mootz was working in his garden in Cincinnati, Ohio, when he saw a single small cloud approaching at a height of about 1,000 feet. It was variegated in pink, red and green, and within seconds he was running indoors for shelter, for an oily liquid resembling blood was falling on him. Wherever a drop fell, on his head, his neck or arms it stung and smarted and he had to wash it off. Next day everything in and around the garden, plants, vegetables, grass and flowers had shrivelled, turned brown and died.

We know that on occasions upward currents of air draw small creatures up into the sky. Tiny hairy caterpillars, wingless ants, beetles and their larvae have all been found drifting at a height of 5,000 feet, and a common flea was once discovered 200 feet up in the air.

But why the fall of hundreds of snakes in a heavy torrent at Memphis, Tennessee, in January, 1877, and several falls of little-known species of dead birds in the streets of Baton Rouge, Louisiana, in 1896? In Châlons-sur-Saône in France in September, 1922, showers of toads fell for two days and on the 12th of June, 1954, hundreds of frogs bounced off open umbrellas when Sutton Park, Birmingham, England, was hit by a freak rainstorm. The same thing happened on a golf course in Arkansas in

January, 1973, when golfers could not believe their eyes on seeing thousands of frogs no larger than a nickel drop from the sky and leap around at their feet. Falls of periwinkles and small fish have been recorded all over the world during the past three centuries. The latest, in April, 1978, comes from Kisanana village in Kenya's Rift Valley where after a two-hour thunderstorm red and black river fish were found scattered over the ground and squirming in the trees. Nobody could account for it, as there is no river in the district and the nearest lake is 14 miles away. "Some villagers think it is a bad omen and others think it is manna from heaven," says local councillor Charles Kiptanui.

Strange seeds have been known to fall from the sky. In 1897 in several towns in the Macerata province in Italy near the Adriatic coast a rain of seeds fell. These, in the first stage of germination, were recognized as seeds of the Judas tree from Central Africa. If a whirlwind had swept them up, the question was why there were no twigs or leaves and why they had all without exception landed in this *one* locality in Italy.

In 1970 in Caldwell, New Jersey, people saw two silvery threads which appeared, converging from different quarters of the sky on Forest and Hillside Avenues. They came down at an angle of 30° to 50° and one ended about 150 feet above the A. P. Smith house, Forest Avenue, while the other hung over a swimming pool not far away.

For a month they remained there, tight and stationary, and seemed undisturbed by several bad electrical storms and winds. Finally on Monday, August 31st, 1970, some of the string dropped to the ground. It was described as translucent and quite stiff, like fibre from a plastic broom.

The material of which the threads were composed was analyzed by DuPont chemical experts, who reported that it was like a Type 6 nylon caprolactan. It was not, they said, of their manufacture. Another sample, turned over to an analytical chemist at Rhode Island University confirmed this, and defined the strings as originally tubelike or hollow in cross-section. To the amazement of the chemists, the strings, after they had been stored for some time in a vacuum chamber, became filled with another substance which defied analysis.

Some of the strangest stories of these unnatural rainstorms occurred in America during the last century. One day in July, 1851, troops at a U.S. army base at Benicia, California, were startled when blood and thin slices of fresh meat showered down on their parade ground. The post surgeon was quoted by the *San Francisco Herald* to the effect that the meat was neatly sliced into pieces about one eighth of an inch thick. In 1869, blood, hairs and strips of flesh fell, again in California, and on March 8th, 1876, flakes of meat were seen by many people floating down out of a clear sky in Kentucky. They were perfectly fresh and were pronounced by an investigator bold enough to eat some of the meat, to taste like mutton or venison. The best explanation that scientists could give, and that not a good one, was that the pieces had been disgorged by a flock of buzzards flying overhead. With knives no doubt!

"If It's Up There . . ."

Nuts, bolts, metal, plastic balls, beads, nails and other man-made articles of all kinds are reported to have been dropped from the sky at various times. In 1968, on four different occasions, mud, chunks of wood, broken glass and pottery rained down out of the sky on the people of Piñar del Rio in Cuba. In the following year on September 3rd, Punta Gorda in Florida had a storm in which a hail of golf balls fell.

Since 1920 it has been tempting to attribute the fall of man-made articles to aircraft, but they have not always been there to take the blame. In November, 1965, a man in Louisville, Kentucky, found that his back yard and the roof of his garage had been sprinkled with bags of cookies, and in April, 1969, a woman driving along a road in Palm Springs, California, had the roof of her car badly dented by a wheel that fell from the sky. In neither of these cases was there a plane near nor did any aircraft report a loss.

The most amazing phenomenon of all is the "natural jackpot"—the shower of money that occasionally falls as it did in Battersea, London, in 1927 in the form of pennies mixed with bits of soda and lumps of coal. On the 30th of September, 1956, children going home from school at Hanham, Bristol, had pennies and halfpennies showered on them from above. In February, 1957, a woman in Gateshead received a shock when two halfpennies whizzed past her, just missing her head, and nobody had been around to throw them. In December, 1968, about 40 to 50 pennies, all bent, came down over Ramsgate, Kent.

"You could not see them falling," said a witness. "All you heard was the sound of them bouncing off the pavement."

On the 6th of January, 1976, some 2,000 marks all in banknotes fluttered down from a clear sky in Limburg, Germany, for two clergymen to pick up—an ideal answer to prayer; and on the 15th of April, 1957, "thousands" of 1,000-franc notes rained down on Bourges, France. Nobody ever claimed them.

The cause? Nobody knows. All that can be said perhaps, is to put an ending to the headline of this section—

"IT'S GOT TO COME DOWN!"

BIZARRE MYSTERIES

The Unexplained

The Plant That Took Over a Garden
The Lethal Fig Tree
The Dreaded Hum
The Singing Teeth
Strange Coincidences
Tweedledum and Tweedledee
A Unique Crossword
A Man in Two Places
The Unknown Correspondent

Mysterious Appearances—

Can the Camera Lie?

—And Disappearances

The Mystery of the Stockholm Ferry
Consumed by Fire
Cases of Premature Cremation
The Case of Mrs. Reeser
No Known Cause

BIZARRE MYSTERIES

THE UNEXPLAINED

The Plant That Took Over a Garden

The mystery may appear in your own back garden as it did in England in the garden of Denis Moat in Canterbury. A gigantic creeper appeared one day with tentacles growing a foot every 24 hours, and huge gourd-like fruits developing. When ripe the gourds weighed some 20 lbs. each and had to be supported on the plant by being put into women's tights hanging from poles. It took several minutes to get one of the fruits open with a knife, and when exposed the flesh of the fruit was white, with pips in the middle.

Soon Mr. Moat's creeper overwhelmed his runner beans and roses and threatened his tomato plants and sprouts. It even menaced the gardens next door. "It's weird," said Mr. Moat. "I've seen on television how plants can take over the world."

In the end the strange plant was referred to a botanist at Kew Gardens who pronounced it to be *Cucurbita fecifolia,* a tropical creeper that had somehow shed its seed and had been carried far from its natural habitat.

Mystery solved!

The Lethal Fig Tree

Some plants and trees may have strange, uncanny properties. From the wall of the 14th century church of St. Newlina in the village of Newlyn East in Cornwall grows an ancient fig tree which nobody, not even the vicar, will touch with shears, pruning-knife or even the hand. It is said to have sprung from the staff that St. Newlina herself stuck here in the ground.

In 1957, the tree was trimmed by William Thomas Phillips, a trapper, Thomas Hoskin, caretaker, and Reginald Glanvill, the church warden. Within a year Phillips died, Hoskin was injured by the falling of a tree, and Glanvill died of a broken heart brought on by the suicide of his son.

In 1964, the Archdeacon of Cornwall, visiting the church, took a leaf from the tree and within a year he too had died as a result of a heart attack.

In 1926, the then vicar had ordered the tree to be trimmed, and he had dropped dead shortly afterwards—a lesson that, some said, ought to have been learned.

Since this is reputed to be a saint's tree, there is no question of exorcism, but the whole series of episodes is both gruesome and inexplicable.

Coincidence? Who knows?

The Dreaded Hum

Of recent years people all over Britain and even abroad have been harassed and given sleepless nights by a persistent humming noise. To those who have heard it, it sounds like a diesel or a ship's engine rising and falling in volume, sometimes getting loud enough to press on the eardrums. Yet there are many, who, because the pitch is so low, cannot hear it at all.

For those who have heard it, the results have been maddening. First reports came from Poole in Dorset in the summer of 1976 and one sufferer there collected the names of 200 others. As a result, scientists became interested.

In the summer of 1977 the nuisance became more

widespread, complaints coming from all parts of the country, from young and old, from city, coast and the countryside. The *Sunday Mirror* received nearly 800 letters from people complaining of loss of sleep, irritability, deteriorating health, inability to read or study, friction between married couples and family rows.

To combat it, one woman in Farnham, Surrey, changed her electric meter three times, altered the supporting brackets to cut down vibration, had her TV aerial down for a week, turned off gas and central heating for three days, moved the freezer out of the kitchen, sealed unused chimney pots, replaced smashed roof tiles and had the house tested three times by acoustic experts. Nothing seemed to work.

One sufferer was reduced to walking the streets, another to driving round for hours, another to keeping a clock whose loud ticking drowned the hum, and another by going temporarily to live with friends. But once back home, the nuisance always took over again.

Where did it come from? Many possible sources were suggested—the street cleaning machines, faulty oxygen pumps in fish tanks and other apparatus, gas or water pressure in the pipes, vibrating TV aerials or phone wires, electric pylons or generators, North Sea gas and oil rigs. Some even believed the hum came from spaceships circling the earth. Others suggested that the cause may have been connected with the person who heard the hum; perhaps the fillings in teeth could act as aerials making signals vibrate through the head and into the ears. But we don't all have fillings. The same applies to blood pressure, inner ear troubles and hardening of the arteries, which were all suggested at times! Not one explanation was satisfactory.

A Member of Parliament to whose notice it was brought asked the Government to investigate, suggesting that it would only cost some tens of thousands of pounds, a small sum compared with the relief many people would obtain. The request was turned down. The head of acoustics in a British university applied to the Science Research Council for a grant for the same purpose, but to no avail.

Presumably the sufferers, unless they can move to places

where they are no longer affected, will still have to bear the discomfort.

Meanwhile the mystery remains.

The Singing Teeth

Radio signals may sometimes be received through strange media. Teeth were suggested as the source of the hum, and there is at least one case in which they actually functioned as a radio receiving set.

This happened to a Florida housewife who had been to her dentist for fillings. Nothing happened until the middle of the night when her husband awakened her complaining that he could hear broadcasting from some station or other. After several nights he began to suspect that her teeth were causing it.

So she went back to her dentist. "Ah," said he, "you must have been sleeping with your mouth open. You see, the mouth can sometimes act as a sort of a baffle box or amplifier, increasing the volume. So keep it closed as much as you can. In any case, don't worry; it'll soon pass off."

It was a hard lot, but the lady did her best and the music became fainter, then ceased altogether. So one day she and her husband decided to invite friends. The evening was passing happily when she suddenly opened her mouth to laugh. Out of it came the theme song from the film "Doctor Zhivago." The company were at first astounded, then applauded in delight. Some of them even danced to the music. So she followed it up with "Rambling Rose."

Happily there is no licence these days for possessing a broadcast receiver. Some of us may be lucky even with our toasters, as was Mrs. Furness of Sydney, Australia, who got an interesting programme one morning while making the breakfast. The drawback was, she burnt the toast.

Strange Coincidences

Would we call coincidences bizarre? Some would certainly merit the name.

Take for instance the cases of the U.S. Presidents. From 1840 every one elected in the 20th year (Harrison 1840, Lincoln 1860, Garfield 1880, McKinley 1900, Harding 1920, Roosevelt 1940 and Kennedy 1960) has died in office. What an omen for the President-to-be of 1980.

There are more startling parallels between Lincoln and Kennedy. Lincoln was first elected to Congress in 1846, Kennedy in 1946. Both had seen military service, both had been champions of civil rights. John Wilkes Booth who assassinated Lincoln was born in 1839, Lee Harvey Oswald who shot Kennedy was born in 1939. Both assassins were Southerners and both were shot in their turn before they could be tried. Booth shot Lincoln in a theatre and fled to a warehouse; Oswald shot Kennedy from a warehouse and fled to a theatre. Both Presidents were shot in the head on a Friday in the presence of their wives. Lincoln was shot in Ford's Theatre, Kennedy in a Lincoln car made by the Ford Company. Lincoln had a secretary named Kennedy who advised him not to visit the theatre; Kennedy had a secretary named Lincoln who advised him against visiting Dallas.

After their deaths they were both succeeded by Southerners named Johnson, Andrew Johnson born in 1808, Lyndon Johnson born in 1908.

Tweedledum and Tweedledee

Quite as bizarre is the story of Wanda Marie Johnson, working as a baggage clerk at Union Station in Washington, and born on the 15th of June, 1953. She became confused in official records with a second Wanda Marie Johnson born on the same day, formerly living in the same district, and both moving later to St. George's, Grenada. Both are mothers of two children; both own 1977 Ford Granadas; both have the same eleven-digit serial number on their social security cards except for the last three digits. Their Maryland drivers' licences are identical because the name and birth date on licences is determined by computer.

So the first Wanda Marie became confused with the second

in medical records, was notified of a debt she didn't owe, received telephone calls from absolute strangers and was ordered to wear glasses while driving though she didn't need them. In December, 1977, she was summoned for not paying a bill to a store she never patronized for furniture she had never bought.

"Don't kid me," said the debt collector. "I've heard plenty of stories like that before."

He knew she was Wanda Johnson, born on the 15th of June, 1953, where she lived and where she worked. There seemed to be no way out.

When she applied for a driver's licence she was told that she already had one with a restriction requiring her to wear the glasses. Four supervisors had to be seen before she could convince them that her sight was perfect. Some days later she received, not one, but two licences.

The confusion was not sorted out until newspaper reporters hit on the story and a meeting between the two Wanda Marie Johnsons was arranged. As a solution the second considered using her maiden name.

A Unique Crossword

When the Allies were planning the Second Front beginning with a projected landing in Normandy in June, 1944, the security officers were shocked by a crossword puzzle that appeared in the *Daily Telegraph*.

The members of M.I.5, the counter-espionage service who were guarding the important secrets were wont to employ some of their spare time working out the solutions to these daily puzzles.

They were surprised one morning before the opening of the campaign to find among the various answers to clues the words OVERLORD, NEPTUNE, UTAH, OMAHA and MULBERRY. Was it pure coincidence or clever espionage that had brought these words into the public eye? Did the Germans know then, that OVERLORD was the code word invented for the whole operation, MULBERRY was the name given to the floating port which was to receive arms and supplies once it was mounted, UTAH and OMAHA were the names given to the two beaches on which the U.S. forces were to land, while NEPTUNE was the code name of the naval support for the whole operation?

If they did, who had betrayed, or was betraying these vital secrets? M.I.5, alarmed, set to work to find out. The compiler of the puzzles was a certain Leonard Dawe, a teacher who lived at Leatherhead in Surrey, England. Why had he chosen these words? Did he have secret information? If so, who were his contacts? If their suspicions were true, the whole invasion project could be in jeopardy.

When faced with the facts Leonard Dawe was indignant. Hadn't a man the right to choose what words he pleased? Anyhow, what did they mean? He hadn't the slightest idea.

The answers he gave to their questions convinced them that Dawe knew nothing of what was happening in the High Command.

One wonders what subtle form of thought transference might have put the words into his head. Or was it just coincidence?

A Man in Two Places

If people in different places can be taken for one, is it possible for one person to be in two places at once? Evidently it is.

In October, 1917, Italian forces facing a combined Austrian and German offensive in Slovenia, now north-west Yugoslavia, were driven back with appalling losses. General Luigi Cadorna, the commander of the Italian forces, was sitting in his tent in despair at the great disaster contemplating suicide, a loaded revolver in his hand. Suddenly at his side appeared the figure of a bearded monk. "Don't be so stupid," it said, and then vanished. General Cadorna, astonished, put aside his pistol.

Years afterwards, when visiting a church in central Italy he recognized one of the monks there as the one who had appeared to him so strangely after the battle. He was doubly confounded when the monk in passing, said softly to him, "You had a lucky escape, my friend." *Yet the monk had never physically left his monastery.*

A similar thing happened 25 years later. Padre Pio, for that was the monk's name, so impressed a Uruguayan gentleman named Damiani that he expressed a hope that when he died it would be in the presence of this remarkable and holy priest.

One night in 1942, when the Archbishop of Montevideo in Uruguay was sleeping, he was suddenly roused by a Capuchin monk unknown to him who urged him to go to the Monsignor Damiani's bedside. He arrived there to find that Damiani had died, and on the bed lay a slip of paper with the message, "Padre Pio came."

This pious Padre Pio, the son of an Italian peasant, carried on his hands, his feet and in his side the *stigmata*, wounds in the same places as those of Christ when he was on the cross. These had come to him years ago, and had remained open, and bleeding. His monastery at Foggia in central Italy was visited by crowds of pilgrims who had heard of this, and nearly £1 million ($2 million) was contributed from all parts of the world to open a hospital there.

Neither the stigmata nor the priest's appearance in two places at the same time has ever been explained.

The Unknown Correspondent

The unknown confronts us at every turn; sometimes we can explain it, sometimes not. There is probably a very good explanation for the experience of Mr. Trevor Silverwood, a former English local councillor and parliamentary candidate, but he would be grateful to anybody who can give it.

For ten years he has been regularly receiving postcards at his home in Bridlington, Yorkshire, and he hasn't the slightest idea who sends them. They are always written in shorthand, always signed by the matchstick figure of the Saint—the hero of the novels of Leslie Charteris—by somebody who seems to know what Mr. Silverwood is doing from day to day, even some of the most intimate details of his private life, and they bear postmarks of places in all parts of the world—India, America, Canada, the Middle East, and from places as near home as Rotherham and Sheffield.

Just before Christmas of 1977 a card, posted in Australia written in the usual shorthand—"JUST FOR YOU," dropped through his letterbox.

"I would dearly like to get my hands on the Big Brother or Sister who is watching me," says Mr. Silverwood. "It was amusing at first, but now no longer." At one time he thought the cards were being sent to these distant places by somebody who knows him well, then sent back with the postmarks on them. This seems an obvious answer, but nothing can be proved.

In October of 1977, weary of receiving the accursed cards, he put an advertisement in his local newspaper begging his unknown correspondent to identify himself. The only answer he had was from Teneriffe telling him not to be naughty, and a Christmas card saying what a good photograph of him the newspaper had published.

"To scare the devil off I let it be known that I was going to the police. Bless me if I didn't get a card from some outlandish place letting me know he knew. I received another from overseas after I had been questioned by the police after a driving matter."

Mr. Silverwood would still be glad if the real correspondent would kindly come forward.

MYSTERIOUS APPEARANCES—

Can the Camera Lie?

There are several instances of photographs having been taken of people invisible to the human eye, some still alive, but others long since dead. For this reason such photographs have been called spirit photographs, and have been investigated by psychic research teams.

One of these teams composed of members of the Royal

Photographic Society carried out an enquiry into the case of Mr. William Hope, a photographic medium in Crewe, England. The leader of the team was Dr. D. L. Johnson who, to make sure that there would be no suspicion of faking, took with him a number of photographic plates bought from many different dealers, and several cameras.

The prints, when they came out, showed not only the medium but many faces of people, some alive, some dead, flower-shapes, clouds and even written messages. The photographers did not even always need to use a camera to get them. Two plates which were held, still in their sealed box, against the subject's head, showed when developed, more written messages.

In the last half-century other examples of such spirit photography have appeared. In 1967, two brothers Richard and Fred Vielleux of Waterville, Maine, took a photograph of a gravestone in the cemetery where both worked as stonemasons, and the resulting print revealed the figure of a small girl standing beside it. They had known her in life before her murder some years previously. This was the first of a remarkable series taken by the two brothers. One was of a plain door, but on the print two faces appeared, both those of the U.S. Marshal, Jeff D. Milton, at two different periods of his life.

White-robed figures often appear; others are monk-like and clad in sombre garments. There are ladies in grey and many representations of Christ, even fairies at the bottom of the garden!

—AND DISAPPEARANCES

The Mystery of the Stockholm Ferry

It was May, 1977, and the 9,000-ton ferry from Helsinki, filled with truckloads of furniture had docked at Stockholm at the end of its 12-hour night journey.

There had been 250 vehicles and 700 passengers on board, and now all had been unloaded and had left the dock except for one lorry whose owner had not appeared to drive it off. The owner was one Juho Heino, a Finnish road hauler, well known to the officers, and he could not be found, nor had he been seen since he had gone to his cabin at midnight.

How had he come to disappear? He was in good health and apparent good spirits when last seen. His business was flourishing and his family circumstances were happy. He was making the crossing to bring the load of furniture to a daughter who is married to a Swede and resident in Stockholm.

What worried and baffled the authorities was that he was the seventh person to vanish completely at sea on that ferry service in the past two years. Three of them had been Swedes, four Finns, and all had disappeared on the same Helsinki-Stockholm run. Not a single body had been recovered nor had any been washed up on shore.

What could have happened to Mr. Heino and the other six passengers? Suicide, at least in his case, was ruled out, and in any event, it would be too much of a coincidence that seven people should commit suicide one after the other on the same boat. And they had certainly not all fallen overboard.

The only conclusion the police could reach was that they had been killed and their bodies disposed of in some mysterious way. "We must assume," said the inspector, "that a crime of some kind has been committed. If we can get to the bottom of Mr. Heino's disappearance we may find an explanation for the other six."

There were two breaks and only two in the pattern. One of the seven had been a woman, and only one of the seven had been found missing while the ferry was still at sea. The disappearance of the others was discovered when the ship was in dock.

Detectives were sent on board for future trips in case of further events of the same kind—a fit job for Leslie Charteris's Saint.

Consumed by Fire

Somehow mysterious episodes seem more convincing when they are connected with the names of famous persons.

J. Temple Thurston was one of the most popular novelists in

England just before and during the First World War. The fact that he was burnt to death was not in the least mysterious, but the way in which it occurred has puzzled experts ever since.

At 2:30 in the morning of the 7th of April, 1919, the famous author was discovered in his room, scorched from the waist down. His clothing had not been touched, and not a single article in the room showed the slightest trace of fire. There was still money in his pockets so the fire could not have been caused to conceal a theft. Mr. Thurston had not called for help nor even moved from his chair and the only fire that was found when the service arrived was not in the room at all, but a blaze outside the door. Nobody could understand why it had started, nor why it did not spread. The whole happening had been silent and mysterious.

At the inquest a verdict was brought in stating that death had been caused by heart failure through inhaling smoke, but the mystery of the "ultra-rapid holocaust," as one investigator put it, was not fathomed.

Cases of Premature Cremation

The phenomena were by no means unknown, for there were cases of people suddenly going up in flames through no apparent cause as far back as the 17th century.

In March, 1908, Margaret Dewar, a retired schoolteacher of Whitley Bay, Northumberland, England, discovered her sister burned to death in a bed, the coverings of which had not been touched by fire. Mr. Eric Russell in 1938 found 19 cases within one year through checking newspaper reports daily.

One night during that year Phyllis Newcombe, a young woman of 22 was dancing with her boy friend on the dance floor of the Shire Hall in Chelmsford, England, when she suddenly caught fire. "As an amazed and horrified crowd looked on, flames suddenly spurted from her body, caught the crinoline-type dress she was wearing and enveloped her." Her friend Henry McAusland tried to beat them out with his bare hands but could do nothing.

It was surmised that somehow a spark from a cigarette might

have caused the fire. At the inquest, however, it was proved that, though dress material identical with that Miss Newcombe had worn would flare up if lit by the flame of a lighter, it would not even ignite from a glowing cigarette end. The coroner vowed that he had never come across a case as mysterious as this, for nobody had seen a cigarette lighter in the hall nor had any fire been near her at the time.

Nearly 20 years later Maybelle Andrews, aged 19, was dancing with her friend Billy Clifford in a Soho night-club in London when flames suddenly burst from her back and chest enveloping all the upper part of her body, igniting her hair. Before anybody could do a thing to help, she had died.

The órigin of the fire was not known. "I saw nobody smoking on the floor," her boy friend said. "There were no candles on the tables and I did not see her dress catch fire from anything. I know it sounds incredible but it appeared to me that the flames burst outwards as if they came from her body."

The coroner's verdict was death from misadventure caused by a fire of unknown origin.

These are only a few of the scores of cases documented. They have even found their way into fiction. Washington Irving, Herman Melville, Balzac, Thomas De Quincey, Zola and Dickens all mention them. Captain Marryatt in *Jacob Faithful* (1833) took a case from the *Times* of the previous year and described it in some detail in his novel. Mark Twain (*Life on the Mississippi,* 1883) described how Jimmy Finn was "not burned in a calaboose but died a natural death in a tan vat, of a combination of delirium tremens and spontaneous combustion."

The Case of Mrs. Reeser

Mrs. Mary Reeser had taken a flat in St. Petersburg, Florida, in order to be near her son who was a doctor there. On July 1st, 1951, she had spent a most enjoyable day with him and his family on the beach and had returned home to have, as she said, an early night. Later she was visited both by her son and by her landlady, Mrs. Carpenter. At the time she was sitting in her easy chair smoking a cigarette. They were the last to see her alive.

At 5 o'clock the next morning Mrs. Carpenter smelt smoke and as a precaution against fire, went into the garage to check, turned off the electric current and, having found nothing suspicious, went back to bed.

At 8 a telegraph boy called with a telegram for Mrs. Reeser. She was not there at the time so Mrs. Carpenter took it and decided to deliver it herself. She went to Mrs. Reeser's door, grasped the knob and started back. It was so hot that it burned her hand. Although there was no smell of burning she shouted for help and her calls were answered by two house-painters who were working on the other side of the street. One of them took a rag in his hand, opened the door and was met by a sudden blast of hot air.

The room was like the inside of an oven; there was some smoke and a small flame spurting from a beam of the partition between it and the kitchen beyond. Mrs. Reeser's bed was empty; she must have fallen asleep in her chair for behind the bed where it should have been were a few coiled springs and the grisly remains of the elderly lady, a piece of the backbone, a skull shrunk to the size of a baseball, a foot encased in a black satin slipper and a small pile of charred ashes, the whole weighing no more than 10 lbs.

Above a height of 4 feet, the covering of the electric wiring had been burnt and candles had been melted though the wicks remained. There were deposits of soot on the internal walls above that height, though below it everything was as it had been except for the immediate vicinity of the remains. A plastic tumbler in the bathroom had been melted, the wood and the shade of the reading lamp had been consumed, the electric clock had stopped at 4:20 in the morning, but when plugged in it went again readily enough.

The whole episode was most mysterious. The gas had been turned off at the wall gas heater and the electric stove had been switched off too. It seemed as if the fire had been intelligent enough to select what had to be burnt, even to the odd object in the bathroom so far away. Though it had almost consumed the body, a pile of newspapers less than a foot away from Mrs.

Reeser's chair which, by all the laws of nature should have been reduced to black ash did not have a single scorch mark on them.

For weeks the case was investigated; by the weather bureau, the police for possible arson, the insurance companies and officials of the public service companies. They found no evidence of petrol, napalm, phosphorus, magnesium—anything that could have caused such a sudden and strange fire as this. Mrs. Reeser's cigarette could not have been the cause even had it been possible for it to ignite her rayon acetate gown, which it was not.

All the explanation that the coroner and the chief of police could offer was that Mrs. Reeser, having taken a couple of sleeping pills, had been overcome by drowsiness while seated in the chair and that by some means her gown had been ignited and the fire had spread. It was unsatisfactory and accounted for hardly anything.

One more to add to the long list of mysteries.

No Known Cause

Events such as these are apt to scare people, and though reports of them appear in the news from time to time, nobody wants to make too much of them beyond acknowledging, as the London coroner and others have done, that the fires are of unknown origin.

In the early 19th century it was believed from the evidence then at hand that victims of spontaneous combustion might be in one or more of five groups—alcoholics or heavy drinkers, elderly women, stout subjects, solitary people and pipe-smokers. Moreover, it was believed that some source of heat was necessary near at hand to make combustion possible. More recent cases have demonstrated that these conditions do not hold.

But it cannot be left at that. Professor Robin Beach of Brooklyn believed that the cause could be electrical, and he persuaded the employees of one factory to step on a metal plate in turn while holding an electrode in the hand. One woman registered 30,000 volts of static and a resistance of half a million ohms. The professor stated that some people can, by walking on carpets in dry weather for instance, build up much more than normal charges and, if they live and work where fire can be generated there can be great danger. It would be quite possible for such a person, after walking some distance on a concrete driveway, to raise the hood of a car, unscrew the caps of a battery, touch off the escaping hydrogen and cause an explosion.

That would be an external cause, but why should fire attack people on dance floors, for instance? One explanation offered is that in certain persons the body absorbs alcohol to saturation, and this could produce spontaneous combustion, but how we do not know. Another is that in certain persons the body chemistry builds up sugars which contain phosphorus. This could result in a highly inflammable condition which could cause the body to burst into flame simply through contact with water, especially perspiration. Once started the tissues would ignite.

Modern investigators, unable to put forward a theory which accords completely with physical science, are thrown back on the paranormal and draw parallels between spontaneous combustion and the rare cases of articles bursting into flame at peak periods of poltergeist activity. If at such times inanimate objects may catch fire, why not a human body?

We do not know. We speculate, we offer this and that explanation and none fits. The mystery remains.

The best thing to do is to treat this extremely rare phenomenon as one would an obscure disease, observe the old recipes for maintaining good and robust health—keep busy, keep your weight down and keep off the bottle.

You may then risk growing old without too much fear of suddenly bursting into flame!

BIZARRE MYSTERIES II

UFO Experiences That Defy Disbelief

The Big Bang of 1908
What Was It?
Has It Been Explained?
"Out of Everywhere into Here"
Discs, Cigars and Doughnuts
Taken Aboard a UFO
The Ordeal of Travis Walton
"They Fly in the Face of Logic"

BIZARRE MYSTERIES II

UFO EXPERIENCES THAT DEFY DISBELIEF

The Big Bang of 1908

On the morning of June 30th, 1908, a train was crossing the vast *taiga* or evergreen forest in the Tungus region of Siberia when, just after 7 o'clock the sky was lit up by a huge glowing mass which streaked northwards towards the horizon. Almost at once a terrific explosion shook the earth as if the whole region had been struck by a gigantic thunderbolt.

Reports of the explosion in the newspapers revealed that whole forests had been uprooted, trees hurled into the air like matchsticks and whole herds of reindeer burnt up or killed by the blast. No human deaths were recorded in this sparsely populated area but some must have occurred, for more than 400 miles away peasants were reported to have been knocked off their feet. At Irkutsk, 550 miles from the middle of the disturbance, the needle of the seismograph went on quivering for more than an hour, and the rumblings from the explosion could be heard more than 600 miles away. Never since the great eruption which had destroyed the Pacific Island of Krakatoa in 1883 had anything so violent as this been witnessed on earth. Not until the atomic bomb which devastated Hiroshima, was anything quite like it to appear again.

What Was It?

Earthquake or volcano was out of the question, for the force which caused the explosion had come, not from inside the earth's crust, but from above, as if some great fireball had been hurled, as it were, out of the sky. Could it have been an enormous meteorite?

It was 13 years before a Russian professor began collecting accounts from eyewitnesses. In 1927 a well-equipped expedition set off into the Tunguska to investigate. Everything they had been told was proved true. As they reached the hub of the disturbance they found the trees progressively damaged and scorched, tops missing and finally black stumps alone remaining. Traces of the vast explosion were everywhere, *but there was no crater*, merely a number of holes in the marshy ground into which they drilled, hoping to unearth pieces of some meteorite or other. Though the search continued on and off for two years, nothing was found.

The mystery remained unsolved.

Has It Been Explained?

For more than 30 years the Soviet Union passed through a trying period of internal troubles, war and subsequent reconstruction. Then in 1961 and 1963 the Academy of Sciences sent another scientist and geophysician, Dr. Aleksei Zolotov, to search for an explanation.

By this time much more was known about nuclear energy, which could now be both detected and measured. It was found that the damage to the trees *had definitely resulted* from a nuclear explosion which equalled, they calculated, that of a ten megaton bomb (i.e. 10,000,000 tons of TNT).

This was obviously something from outer space which did not penetrate the earth's crust as a meteorite would have done.

In 1964 two writers, Altov and Shurateva, ventured a novel explanation in an article published in a Leningrad journal. Was it not possible that the Krakatoa volcano, which could have been seen from outer space by intelligent beings equipped with the right apparatus, was taken by them to be a light signal from earth? In terms of the universe, light travels but slowly, and it might well be 25 years before an answer could arrive from some part of outer space in the form of a laser beam. But this beam directed at our earth may have turned out to be too strong, and, instead of transmitting a signal, was transformed into matter on contacting our atmosphere, swooped down in a huge flaming mass, being burnt up in the course of its transit, and on reaching earth its remnant devastated hundreds of square miles of forest land.

Ingenious, but improbable.

Now another Soviet scientist has stated that, in his opinion, this was a nuclear explosion which could only have been caused by a spacecraft from another part of the universe colliding with earth—in other words, a UFO—an unidentified flying object.

"Out of Everywhere into Here"

As far as man's conception of his relation with the universe is concerned, humanity seems to have passed through two stages and is now entering a third.

The first stage was during the lengthy ancient and medieval periods when it was generally believed that the earth was the focal point of all created things, sun and stars moving round it, and everything on, below and above it created for the service and delight of man. This conception was rudely shattered by Copernicus who proved that far from being the focus, the earth was only one of the many smaller bodies circling the sun, and that the sun was only one of thousands of fixed stars.

Man was thus relegated from his superior status in creation to a much lower one, but he could still regard himself as being the highest form of life on this earth, which was thought to be the only place in the universe where life existed. This was the second stage. Nobody even imagined that there could be living beings anywhere but here; the very idea was absurd. More's *Utopia*, Bacon's *New Atlantis*, Harrington's *Oceana* and all the strange places visited by Dean Swift's Gulliver were imagined to be somewhere on this earth.

Only towards the end of the last century and in this has it dawned on man that there may be beings, possibly more intelligent than we are, dwelling on other planets, possibly planets circling other fixed stars, and that these beings may not only have been trying to contact us, but may even have set foot on earth long before human civilization matured, if indeed it has yet done so! It is roughly only during the last half-century that space travel has been thought remotely possible but, like all other novel ideas, once the human mind grasped it, there has been no stopping the flood of enquiry, liberally mixed with fantasy that has not only furnished us with particulars of more than 12,000 sightings of unidentified flying objects, but has created a completely new field of research, as well as a new *genre* of modern literature—the vast province of science fiction.

This is the third stage. To the advanced thinker of today life is a principle of the universe, just as firmly rooted as force and matter. Even to the most obstinate scientist or religious extremist, it is now inconceivable that on the millions of planets on which life could be possible, it does not in fact exist.

Two astronomers, Carl Sagan and Frank Drake, estimate that, on the planets surrounding the 200,000,000,000 stars in our galaxy alone, there are "a million civilizations at or beyond the earth's present level of technological development." Sebastian von Hoerner of the National Radio Astronomy Observatory adds, "I seriously think that trying to establish contact with other beings in the universe is our next great task."

Discs, Cigars and Doughnuts

Up to 1945 the attention of the bulk of mankind was too occupied with the problem of survival to worry much about anything else. It was not until two years later that the first reports of strange flying objects began to come in and set people wondering what they could be.

In 1953 the Kinross Air Base in Michigan picked up one on their radar screen. It was chased for some 160 miles by a military jet aircraft, then both aircraft and flying object vanished, leaving no trace. In May, 1954, people at Canberra, Australia, saw another such large shining object going northwards in the sky. It appeared to be lurching strangely, when another similar object, dark red, rushed towards it and both instantly vanished.

Even then, serious investigation might not have taken place had not these Unidentified Flying Objects apparently forced themselves on the attention of people all over the world. It started in Alabama with the still unexplained experience of an Air Force colonel, William Coleman. His report later disappeared from government files, but he still recollects the incident.

"Visibility was between 46 and 50 miles that day. We were just south of Montgomery, Alabama, and I was leaning back to relax for a few minutes while the co-pilot flew the plane. That's when I first saw the object, up to 10,000 feet above me, travelling in the same direction we were, at about the 2 o'clock position.

"I asked the co-pilot if he saw the shiny white object and he said he did—that it must be a craze in the windshield. So I took the airplane and started to turn. The craze should either have disappeared or fallen off to the side. But it didn't clear up. The object began to descend and it crossed our altitude.

"It was an odd-looking thing. There was no sign of any wings or a vertical stabilizer. We started to close on it—within a mile now, and coming up on the tops of trees pretty fast. When we came within three-fourths of a mile I could see it was definitely a circular object.

"At one-eighth of a mile I told the crew: 'Keep your heads cool. We are going to overtake it and I want you to capture every detail that you can.' Naturally no one had a camera.

"After a few more manoeuvres the object suddenly disappeared."

He later asked the crew not to discuss the incident with anybody until each had written his report. When the reports were given in they agreed in every detail. The object was about 60 feet across and 10 feet thick in the middle, it was circular and had no sharp edges, no seams, no rivet marks and no windows.

It was the shade titanium (i.e. greyish with a metallic lustre) and had lights. It was, according to Coleman, "something that no known technology on earth could have produced."

From that time, reports came in more frequently. In April, 1964, a policeman named Zamora described as "an intelligent and respected officer" told how he had seen an egg-shaped UFO land in the desert outside Socorro in New Mexico and then take off shortly afterwards with a sort of bluish-white, roaring flame. The incident, in spite of appeals, was never thoroughly investigated.

In September of the following year a policeman in New Hampshire approached a car whose driver, a woman, refused to drive on because she had been terrified by a huge flying object which had followed her for 10 miles. The policeman refused to believe her until the story was confirmed by a young man who had been forced by it to hide in a ditch. On the way home not only the policeman but *fifty other* people saw the intensely glowing object which lit up the whole area.

Almost at the same time a series of disturbing events was happening all over the world. A Mr. Howell of Texas, driving home one summer evening, saw a bluish light overhead which bathed his car in a blue haze, then shot off at a tangent in a burst of speed. Mr. Terry Pell of Spalding, Lincolnshire, England, saw a red light floating about 50 yards in front of the lorry he was driving. It looked like the large headlight of a car or an enormous human eye. Mrs. Rachel Atwill, living a few miles away, awakened by a loud droning noise, saw the same kind of floating, flickering light of some sort of aircraft, dome-shaped on top.

Taken Aboard a UFO

By the end of the sixties this kind of phenomenon was well known and more startling reports had come in of people who had actually seen the figures, and there was one case of a married couple who had apparently been taken aboard one of the spaceships.

The full story, improbable and bizarre though it may seem, was only revealed under hypnosis.

Mr. and Mrs. Hill were a couple from Portsmouth, New Hampshire, on a visit to Canada in September, 1961. Driving late one night towards the town of Lancaster, New Brunswick, they noticed a peculiar light moving over the treetops a little way off. Mr. Hill got out, taking his binoculars. When he looked through them he was amazed to see a pancake-shaped object with a row of windows along the rim and behind them, moving figures. Terrified, he ran back to the car and then sped off towards home.

What happened during the months which followed was even more strange. They both became subject to anxiety states and Mrs. Hill had repeated nightmares in which she was abducted by beings not of this earth. They told their story to experts belonging to the National Investigations Committee on Aerial Phenomena. What puzzled them all was, if the Hills had only *seen* the UFO and had then hurried home, they should have arrived at about 3 a.m. whereas they did not arrive until 5. How had the hours not accounted for been spent?

When the two agreed to be hypnotized separately an amazing sequence of events was laid bare. It appeared that, shortly after they had driven away from the place where Mr. Hill had seen the UFO, their car had been stopped by creatures from outer space who took possession of their minds and, inside the UFO, subjected them to a detailed physical examination in which they were scanned and probed with instruments, and fragments of their skin, hair and fingernails removed. One of the examiners inserted a long needle into Mrs. Hill's abdomen. When it caused her pain, he passed his hand over her eyes and the pain ceased.

The examiners were described by Mrs. Hill under hypnosis as having grey skin, small slits for mouths, large and curiously elongated heads, almond-shaped eyes and hands with three fingers. In one of the sessions Mrs. Hill actually described the small room in which the examination had taken place, and the star map which the extra-terrestrial visitors used to guide them about the universe.

What is one to make of such a story as this? Dr. Benjamin Simon who treated the couple explained. "It must be understood that hypnosis is a pathway to the truth *as it is felt and understood by the patient.* The truth is what he believes to be the truth, and this may or may not be consonant with the ultimate, non-personal truth. Most frequently it is."

The Ordeal of Travis Walton

We must make what we can of the story told by the Hill couple, though more light may be thrown on it by a second bizarre event which took place at Snowflake, Arizona, on November 5th, 1975, when 22-year-old Travis Walton with five mates was driving home after a long day's work in the woods. Suddenly one of them shouted, "Look, there's a flying saucer just above the trees!"

The truck screeched to a halt and young Walton hurriedly jumped out and ran towards the spot to investigate. Suddenly there was a bright blue flash and Walton was knocked to the ground. Terrified, the lads in the truck made off. When, ten minutes later, they had plucked up enough courage to return to the spot neither Walton nor the mysterious flying object could be seen.

The matter had to be reported to the Navajo County Sheriff Martin Gillespie who immediately suspected a hoax. But when Walton could not be found the matter became serious enough to warrant a murder investigation. Lie detectors were used, but nothing the lads said was enough to justify charges being brought, so Walton had to be listed as a missing person. The woods were thoroughly combed on foot and horseback, and even with helicopters, but nothing whatever turned up.

Then, five days later, Walton suddenly reappeared in the village of Heber, a few miles from Snowflake. He was pale, shocked and 10 lbs. lighter in weight than he had been before his disappearance. The story he told was hair-raising.

"As I got near to the UFO something hit me. It was like an electric shock in my jaw and everything went black.

When I awoke I thought I was in a hospital. I was on a table in a big room with a bright light in my eyes. Then, as my eyes focused I saw three figures. They weren't human. They were about five feet tall and wore tight-fitting brown robes. Their skin was white. They had domed foreheads, no hair, and their eyes were very big. They just peered at me and nobody made a sound.

"A man in a blue uniform appeared and led me into another room. He seemed human but he wore a helmet like a fishbowl. I sat in a high-backed chair with buttons on one arm and a lever on another. Outside it was dark and I could see only stars. I pushed the lever and the scene changed. I was scared to touch anything else in case we were in a spaceship.

"Eventually I was led down a ramp into a kind of hangar with some small flying saucers nearby. Three more human-looking people appeared, one of them a woman. I was angry and shouting questions but they never spoke. They laid me on a table and put a mask on my face. It was like an oxygen mask with a big black ball on top. I seemed to lose consciousness.

"When I awoke I was on the side of the road. I ran and ran until I came to a phone booth. I realized I was in Heber."

The accounts are bizarre, but constant repetition, even of the bizarre, can become monotonous and commonplace. People are in a car, they see what they think is a UFO, it draws nearer, the engine stops, they cannot start it; they stare at a humanoid, in some cases they lose the sense of time, are taken inside the craft, see creatures varying in appearance with each story, but there is a sameness about them. One has a feeling of having read the same sort of story so many times before.

"They Fly in the Face of Logic"

Officialdom continues to play down the whole business. Even the Air Force, some of whose members have had experiences of one kind or another, does not consider UFO's to be a valid subject of study, though an official textbook used between 1972 and 1974 stated that "the world must face the unpleasant possibility of alien visitors to our planet or at least of alien-controlled UFO's."

Up to 1969 the U.S. Government collected in Project Blue Book evidence of the existence of such objects, and this has recently been published, though some accounts, including ex-Colonel William Coleman's first sighting of 1954, are missing. In 1969, the conclusion was announced that there was no hard evidence that UFO's were anything but natural phenomena. In December 1977, the United Nations began a debate on a proposal to establish a special world-wide agency to study reports, but the U.S. Government turned down the White House request to open an official enquiry. Yet it has budgeted about $21 million over the next seven years for a project called Search for Extra-Terrestrial Intelligence (SETI).

Thousands of people are convinced believers, but one observer who takes a surprisingly hard-nosed view of all this is Isaac Asimov, the biochemist turned author whose original science fiction is known and read the world over.

"Eyewitness reports of actual spaceships and actual extra-terrestrials are in themselves totally unreliable," he says. "An unidentified flying object is just that. Unidentified."

To this we would add—yes but they are still objects and *must be explained.* Sometimes the explanations—especially of UFO phenomena—are even more bizarre than the phenomena themselves!

INDEX